Images of
Alcoholism

edited by
Jim Cook
Mike Lewington

1979

 **AEC**

Published jointly by the Educational Advisory Service, British Film Institute,
127 Charing Cross Road, London WC2H 0EA and the Alcohol Education
Centre, the Maudsley Hospital, 99 Denmark Hill, London SE5 8AZ

The Editors

Jim Cook is Teacher Adviser in the Educational Advisory Service of the British Film Institute.
Mike Lewington is Course Co-ordinator at the Alcohol Education Centre, London, and a group supervisor for the Alcohol Counselling Service.

The Contributors

Edward Buscombe is Editor of Publications in the Educational Advisory Service of the British Film Institute.
Richard Dyer is Lecturer in Film at the University of Warwick.
Marcus Grant is the Director of the Alcohol Education Centre.
Judith Harwin lectures in Social Work at the London School of Economics and is Educational Therapist at the Newington Unit, Ticehurst.
Jim Hillier lectures in Film at Bulmershe College of Higher Education.
Roger King is Senior Lecturer in Communications and the Sociology of Literature at the Polytechnic of the South Bank.
Shirley Otto is Co-Director of the Detoxification Evaluation Project and is Chairperson of the Camberwell Council on Alcoholism.
Bruce Ritson is Consultant Psychiatrist at the Unit for the Treatment of Alcoholism, Royal Edinburgh Hospital.
Andrew Tudor is Senior Lecturer in Sociology at the University of York.

ISBN 0 85170 091 8

(Cover: *The Lost Weekend,* USA 1945, Dir. Billy Wilder)

Acknowledgements

The editors would like to thank the following: Marcus Grant, Director of the Alcohol Education Centre, for his continuing support; Phillipa Hayes for typing the manuscript; Jim Hillier for his substantial contribution to the overall conception of the Conference, the NFT Season and this publication; David Seligman for his assistance with the initial compilation of films about alcoholism; the BFI Stills Section; Erich Sargent for shooting the television stills; and finally the individual contributors of the papers to the Conference and the essays to this publication.

Contents

Foreword

by Mike Lewington

The popularly perceived synonymity of 'drinking problems' and skidrowism or the exhibition of flamboyant symptoms inevitably entails a likelihood of failure to recognise or interpret problems experienced as being related to the pattern of alcohol consumption on the part of the individual or members of the helping professions with whom they are involved. That such a failure of recognition exists has been established at national level by the huge difference evident between the number of people presenting to agencies with alcohol problems of various kinds and the estimated number of people experiencing alcohol problems: in 1975, 14,000 and 400,000 respectively (England and Wales). On a more individual level, Shaw *et al.*[1] commenting on a 1974 General Population Survey note that:

> Most people considered themselves 'normal drinkers' and normal drinking was approved. An analysis of respondents who reported that they had been 'criticised' for their drinking or who had been 'advised to cut down' showed that they were no more likely than other respondents to define themselves as having 'drinking problems' or to have sought help for drinking problems.
>
> Each of the respondents was asked if they had suffered any of a list of fifteen specific problems caused by drinking. . . . Ten respondents reported having experienced five or more of the problems and nine of these reported having been 'criticised' and eight being 'advised to cut down'. None of this, at least at the time of interview, seemed to have much bearing on their self-definition. None of them considered themselves to be 'problem drinkers' or 'alcoholics' or overtly wanted help. Indeed, whatever characterisation one extracted from the general population, be it persons defining themselves as having problems, persons reporting experiencing alcohol related problems or persons reporting a consumption level way above average, none of these persons saw themselves as 'alcoholics' and only a minority of four saw themselves as being heavy drinkers.

Why this situation should occur has never been seriously examined by researchers, who have preferred to concentrate on the failure of members of the helping professions to recognise the implication of alcohol in physical, psychological and social problems presented by clients, rather than examine why this connection has not been made by the clients themselves. Anecdotally, this phenomenon is often explained by recourse to notions about alcoholism being a 'disease of denial'—one of the pseudo-scientific beliefs that became popular through the offices of Alcoholics Anonymous and a medical profession that sought to legitimise its disease model orthodoxy in the period around World War Two.

A more useful approach may be to consider the phenomenon as a conflict of definitions of what constitutes 'an alcohol problem' or 'alcoholism'; a conflict between those definitions espoused by the helping professions and those of the general public. This issue is particularly important at the present time, when the distance between these definitions is widening.

From an alcohologist's point of view, the aim of the conference, the proceedings of which are condensed into this volume, was to attempt to account for those popular views of alcoholism by an examination of the dominant images and models informing the representation of alcoholism in cinema and television and a consideration of how these representations work to reinforce and reflect commonsense 'knowledge' about the condition.

We were conscious that previously those concerned with alcohol problems, and particularly with prevention and health education, had confined expression of their concern with the media to matters of alcohol advertising and the quantity and frequency of alcoholic beverage consumption in television programmes. Our concern was rather to initiate a mapping out of the features of the alcoholic stereotype and to consider its function in these media and in society at large, and to examine the implications of its operation for the general public, treatment agencies and those involved in utilising these media for preventive and educational strategies.

The success or otherwise of the venture may be judged in terms of the quality with which this debate continues.

Notes

[1] S. Shaw *et al.*, *Responding to Drinking Problems*, Croom Helm, 1978.

Introduction

by Jim Cook

The series of essays in this book are revisions of papers given at a week-long conference held at the National Film Theatre in September 1978 on 'The Representation of Alcoholism in Cinema and Television'. Although the Conference, organised jointly by members of the Educational Advisory Service of the British Film Institute and the Alcohol Education Centre, had as its target audience 'professionals' from health education, media studies, and the television institutions, the intention was to make its concerns available to a wider constituency and consequently a season of films on 'Representations of Alcoholism' was programmed at the NFT concurrently with the Conference.

This publication is designed to pursue further those dual aims: i.e. both to offer the various and differentially concerned professional interests some initial and tentative case-study accounts around the problematic of 'representation' and 'effects', and to present these accounts in such a way that they do not become the exclusive prerogative of 'specialists'. In relation to this latter point it is worth noting that contributors are drawn equally from media studies and alcohol education—a factor which accounts for the book having perhaps less of a formally consensual homogeneity than it would have had if it had been written by people drawn exclusively from one or other of the two areas.

We believe that such value as the book has lies precisely in its bringing together, around a common theme, considerations of that theme from a generally shared perspective but also from institutionally very different starting points. This shared perspective is important. For behind the particular instance under scrutiny in this book there are more general considerations at stake. Firstly how best can the complex processes which operate to define socially various groups within our society be thought through, and secondly (and possibly more importantly) if it is deemed that those definitions are inadequate, how can they be changed? Within this perspective this book is intended as a modest but serious contribution to that small but growing body of work which, although originating in a variety of different 'disciplines', takes upon itself the urgent political task of trying to account for current dominant images of class, race, gender, role, attribute, etc.

Those images are here refracted through the representation of the alcoholic and through images of the social activity of drinking. To context them further this Introduction concludes by cross-referring points made in the NFT Programme Booklet's introduction to the season with the particular concerns of the essays in this book.

The essays by Andrew Tudor and Richard Dyer which form the first part are intended to pick up on the more general concerns and to inflect them towards representations of alcoholism: 'by representation we mean a concern with the modes—narrative conventions, stereotyping, etc.—through which certain models and meanings are mediated and kept in circulation in society.' Seeking 'to oppose simple notions about films merely reflecting real life' the essays critically 'read' the dominant tradition of media effects studies (Tudor), and suggest more culturally sophisticated models for understanding how 'human society and individuals within it make sense of that society through generalities, patternings and typifications' (Dyer).

The second part of the book considers filmic representations in more detail. By looking at how films from the 1930s to the 1970s '"illustrate" at one level changes in the "explanations" for alcoholism and treatment of it', Mike Lewington demonstrates how although certain broad changes in the models for understanding alcoholism as a phenomenon have been picked up in the films, the range of representations is in fact extremely limited. He concludes inevitably that dominant representations seem to derive far more from dramatic and ideological imperatives than from a desire to adequately represent the socio-cultural reality of the phenomenon and the attendant sets of understandings of it.

The other three essays in this section, by Marcus Grant, by Judith Harwin and Shirley Otto and by Bruce Ritson pick up on this conclusion and with varying emphases detail its implications in relation to the representations respectively of the alcoholic hero, women alcoholics, and treatment agencies. It is important to stress here that none of the emphases are thematic ones but rather start from a position that all cultural artefacts thematise or encode (and thus work to transform) their 'data' i.e. the raw material of socially constructed actuality. As the Introduction to the NFT season put it: 'it [the season] seeks to ask what are the themes implied by forms and choices of representation ... [and] ... what is the ideological work of these films in relation to the "facts" about and attitudes towards alcoholism.' Common to all of the essays in this section is a concern with 'the tensions present in all the films (and perhaps all films) between covert meanings derived from the form, and more explicit ones at the level of plot. The tensions provoke many questions: why do the representations emphasise suffering, degradation, violence?; how are women alcoholics portrayed differently from men?; why (as seems to be the case) is the rehabilitation of women alcoholics represented more accurately than with the male hero figures?; to what extent have the films a mythological dimension in which alcohol (like drugs more recently) is only a dramatic "function" in stories whose deep structure is a series of complex reflections on the possibilities and problems of individual independence and self-control in a "world" reduced to a choice between conformity and transgression?'

Using the insights and tentative hypotheses derived from cinema's more extreme representations—alcoholism rather than social drinking—the third part considers the pervasive but more oblique TV representations of social drinking. Why the two institutions should approach drinking differently is not directly considered in the two essays' specific accounts of *Hazell* and *Coronation Street/ Crossroads*. However, their stress on the commitment of television (in these instances through the series format) to *regularly entertain* does by implication point to a general mode of operation which is different from that of cinema with its, broadly, *one-off commitment to appeal,* and which would repay further research. Edward Buscombe's piece on *Hazell* demonstrates how a stereotype of a certain type of alcoholic, used exclusively for dramatic purposes, can nonetheless at certain points almost as an aside reveal through its concentration on fictional modes more about the alcoholic condition than any amount of head-on realistic accounts. Roger King, given the nature of his material, develops this point even further and shows how *Coronation Street* and *Crossroads* use drinking mythopoeically to account symbolically for aspects of social life.

Finally in the last part Mike Lewington picks up on the consistent theme running through so many of the essays—namely that effects cannot simply be read off from 'realist' content—and considers the implications of this for Health Education films. We consider it appropriate that a book whose overall concern is with the use of representations should stop at this point where it opens out its tentative conclusions for a more general consideration.

Oblique - slanting, indirect

Part One: Theoretical Perspectives

On Alcohol and the Mystique of Media Effects

by Andrew Tudor

It has long been claimed that the media can encourage people into acts that they would otherwise not consider and into beliefs that they would otherwise not espouse. Indeed, part of the force with which the Hollywood self-censorship agency, the Hays Office, was able to apply its famous Production Code stemmed from a growing fear of media effects, and in the 1934 formulation of the Code (that is, the year after Prohibition was repealed) it is notable that alcohol still finds a mention. Though the Code's formulation was hardly a tight piece of drafting—'the use of liquor in American life, when not required by the plot or for proper characterisation, will not be shown'—the very appearance of alcohol along with sex, crime, obscenity and profanity suggests that its movie presentation was taken very seriously.

Yet among the countless effects studies conducted since the thirties, hardly any have been concerned with the effects of the media on alcohol consumption. Perhaps too many vested interests are involved. But it is still widely claimed that the mass media are responsible for much else that is wrong in our society, a belief given constant currency by the media themselves. Thus we periodically find ourselves embroiled in what Stan Cohen has called 'moral panics': times at which the news-media, in particular, amplify certain topics into issues of apparently enormous public conern.[1] When such 'panics' focus on the role of the media themselves (where violence and sex are the favourite topics) they presuppose the truth of the view that the media effect us simply and directly, whatever our individual commitments and characters.

I find that hard to accept. Although the media are certainly not guiltless, they do not cause us to act in specific ways or to believe in certain things simply by virtue of the fact of their media presentation. The influence that the media can exert over social behaviour cannot be understood in such simple terms. Yet, in public discussion we persist in talking about media effects as if they are well understood, although remarkably few effects studies could be said to have conclusively demonstrated anything at all. To understand how that has come to be so, and to consider the alternatives if we are sensibly to explore the representation of alcoholism, it is necessary to know something of the history of media research. It is a large topic, and there are a number of useful summaries available; here I shall limit myself to something of a potted history.[2] For convenience I divide it into four periods: 1925–1940; 1940–1960; 1960–1970; and 1970 onward.

6

On Media Research
(i) 1925—1940
It was in this period that the mass audience for cinema and radio expanded beyond all expectations, a development which in consequence occasioned a good deal of public discussion. Much argument revolved around the adverse effects movies were presumed to be having upon children and upon certain classes of adult who, it was implied, were less discriminating than more distanced observers of the cultural scene. Often that concern found highly moralistic expression (the Legion of Decency were responsible for the 1934 Production Code) taking for granted that the movies did indeed have unfortunate effects. In that respect, of course, the pattern remains the same today. Organisations like the National Viewers and Listeners Association still start by assuming media effects, even though the accumulated evidence of half-a-century of research hardly permits such simple generalisations.

In the thirties, however, there was no accumulation of research, and it was as a result of concern about the effects of motion pictures upon children and adolescents that there emerged the first major systematic attempt to assess the impact of the movies. These researches were collectively known as the Payne Fund Studies, and ultimately reported in a dozen volumes covering topics as varied as attitude change, emotional responses, effects on sleep patterns, and juvenile delinquency. Some were based on experiments, some on survey work, yet others on extended interviews. Not surprisingly, given their assumptions, they came down on the side of those who believed that the cinema was having serious effects (*Our Movie Made Children* ran the title of the popular summary volume) and they generally emphasised adverse effects rather than beneficial ones.[3]

Of course their conclusions now need serious qualification. Several of the studies are methodologically suspect, and most of them suffered from their emphasis on individual effects at the cost of neglecting the social contexts in which the movies featured. In that, however, they followed the characteristic thinking of the period. These years saw the beginning of a development of a view of modern society—later to be christened Mass Society—in which the mass media were conceived to be undermining, even replacing, traditional patterns of social relations. People in mass society, it was suggested, were becoming isolated anonymous automatons—reflex products of the media. It was an image of social life that dovetailed neatly with the idea that the media affected people directly, regardless of the socio-cultural world in which they lived, and it was this account that was to dominate thinking about the media for almost thirty years.

(ii) 1940—1960
By the mid-fifties the Mass Society theory was at its most influential, an unquestionable and unquestioned framework. The essence of the view is well expressed in this passage from C. Wright Mills:

(1) the media tell the man in the mass who he is—they give him identity;

(2) they tell him what he wants to be—they give him aspirations; (3) they tell him how to get that way—they give him technique; and (4) they tell him how to feel that way even when he is not—they give him escape.[4]

To all intents and purposes society was now Mass Society, and the process of communication a one-way hypodermic injection into the vein of the body politic. Whoever they were, wherever they were, the media of mass communication affected all its uncritical consumers equally.

Yet even in this, the finest hour of the Mass Society researches, there was work in progress which would ultimately render the master image suspect. The war had generated considerable interest in propaganda and, especially in America, there were attempts to assess the effects of different sorts of propaganda material.[5] The net result was increasing recognition that the 'effect' of a particular item was not a simple linear consequence of the content of the item itself. Selective perception (perception conditioned by the predispositions of audience members) proved far more important than Mass Society theory suggested. Researchers found people perversely able to interpret what they saw or heard in line with their own already established beliefs; they were rarely passive recipients of media messages. Nor were they the social isolates, the anonymous 'faces in the crowd' of the fifties. Mass society had not replaced localised group structure with a world of isolated individuals—easy game for the carnivorous media. Social life had changed, certainly, but groups still existed, people still interacted. The media reached them, if at all, via a network of social relations; it may have been different to traditional patterns, but it wasn't necessarily inferior.[6]

By the end of the fifties such deviations from the orthodoxy were demanding more and more attention. Though the dominant perspective still emphasised direct effects on individual subjects, there was now a growing body of research which, at the very least, was inconclusive about media effects.

(iii) 1960—1970

It was during these ten years that media researchers recognised that their failure to arrive at convincing findings was a result of the way in which they had conceptualised 'effects' rather than a failing in research technique. In 1960 a major review of the current state of effects research could put it no stronger than this: 'mass communication does not ordinarily serve as a necessary and sufficient cause of audience effects, but rather functions through a nexus of mediating factors.'[7] The problem now was to establish the mediating factors and so generate a new and less restrictive model of the process of mass communication. All the time and money invested in traditional effects research had produced only confusion.

Recognising the need to rethink the problem, however, was not the same as rethinking it. A new understanding of the relation between media and society was not immediately forthcoming; understandably, researchers first tried modifications of existing approaches. The so-called 'laissez-faire' view became popular (particularly among those working in the media) in which the media were no longer seen to play the manipulative role allocated to them in the Mass Society theories. Instead, they were said to provide a wide range of cultural materials from which people chose what best suited them. In a real sense the people were 'given what they want'. The school of research most closely related to this rationalisation was dubbed the 'uses and gratifications' approach. Audiences were studied from the point of view of the *use* they made of media products to gratify particular needs: the emphasis being on the active audience which avoided the traditional passivity and isolation assumptions. Descendants of that style of research still thrive, and have indeed arrived at a richer understanding of the social-psychological functions of the media. But in recent years yet another model of media effects has begun to emerge, this time asking a different set of questions and in more general social terms.

(iv) 1970 onward

Perhaps the easiest way to appreciate the change is to contrast the traditional 'effects' emphasis with some of the common features of more recent perspectives. The old effects studies focused on specified effects on individuals who, if not in experimentally simulated isolation, were selected so as to minimise the impact of their individuality and social background. In its crudest versions this approach produced almost no serious evidence of media effects. In the hands of more imaginative researchers it did produce some evidence, but even then the effects thus isolated were highly mediated and barely identifiable within the conventional before/after methodology. Even on the most extensively research topic, screen violence, the modest results of effects studies could hardly be generalised beyond laboratory restrictions.[8]

To this day researchers can rarely agree on the precise significance of television and movie violence. Yet common sense urges that all those violent battles and chases must be of some significance; if traditional effects studies can tell us little about it, then what can? It is in answer to that sort of question that some recent work has emphasised what I shall call the 'cultural effect'. On screen violence, for instance, this leads to two key assertions. First, that what is at issue is not simply the incidence of violence, but also the various contexts in which it features. Thus, in analysing representations of violence in the media we would need to ask *detailed* questions about the kinds of narrative in which it features, about the stereotypes and character typifications to which it relates, and about the media-constructed 'worlds' in which it appears. This, in combination with systematic audience analysis, would lead us to a much better understanding of the meaning media violence has for those who see it. Secondly, that it is not the single before/after effect which is significant, but the more general consequences of patterned repetition. Hence the well known 'desensitisation' argument: the claim that constant exposure to media violence desensitises us to the real thing. Behind that lies the more general claim that repeated patterns of action, familiar narratives or typical images can be significant in ways not immediately discernable to those concerned with effects at an individual level.

I have called this the 'cultural effects' approach because it leads us to ask how the world-views and stereotypes found in the media affect the cultural frameworks we use to understand our everyday world. The media provide us with a sort of 'cultural reservoir' which, directly and indirectly, influences what is taken for granted in our society. By providing us with the terms within which we comprehend the world around us, the media tend along with other agencies actually to constitute that world. It's a very different emphasis to that found in the traditional concept of 'effects', and it leads to very different styles of research. Such analysis would, for instance, require a far more comprehensive and systematic understanding of media representations themselves (and the 'languages' in which they are cast) as well as demanding that we conceive the media as articulators of our cultures rather than as sources of individual effects. Four decades of effects research have not delivered the goods. That does not mean—as some have suggested—that the media have no effects. It means that the effects that they do have are not those which researchers have traditionally sought. The virtue of the cultural effects approaches (and there are many different variants currently available) is that they take this failing of media research seriously, and try to develop a new analysis which will overcome it.

On Cultural Effects

What sorts of questions, then, should one be asking? In general I think there are two major areas to which we must pay attention: they might be termed 'world construction' and 'world maintenance'.[9]

(i) world construction

Here we are dealing primarily with learning or socialisation and hence particularly with the impact of the media on children and adolescents. To them the media offer an almost infinitely expandable peer group, a formidable addition to family, school, and friends, through which ways of understanding the world and of mapping its features are provided along with dramatic models of what will count as appropriate behaviour. Note that this isn't necessarily a consciously articulated process; these are aspects of our lives that, in the very social nature of things, we come to take for granted. Such socialisation involves first learning how to act in society, and then unlearning the fact that this was a lesson in the first place. So it is not the most obvious questions I am proposing here—what effects will the violence in this movie have on an audience of 14 year olds?—but rather: if coercive forms of social interaction are repeatedly shown to be the norm and to be functional for the individual 'hero', will resort to coercion become an established part of our culture and hence naturalised, made an unquestionable feature of 'human nature'? Over time we do learn frameworks from the media, ways of seeing. And when we have learned them we conveniently forget that they are learned. They come to be seen as 'common sense' or 'what everybody knows'. They are no longer recognised for what they are: partial, learned frameworks which relate to particular interests and generate particular points of view. Instead, they become the constants of our cognitive processes, the fundamental assumptions on which we rest our sense of an ordered social life. In that way they become part of the very constitution of the world as we see it.

10

(ii) world maintenance
For adults, whose basic frameworks are already established, the problem is to legitimate or maintain the world as they see it. Accordingly, what we choose to watch or read—itself limited severely by what is made available to us—helps to define a tacit range of consensus, setting the boundaries of our toleration by labelling as deviant certain roles, attitudes, and activities. It isn't necessarily a matter of conspiracy, though it may be. In large part those who control the media are as much captives of past learning as we are; they can, in all honesty, maintain their own claims to integrity and independence while still maintaining us in our basic conceptions of the world. Indeed, they are almost obliged to do so. If they are to be intelligible to so many of us they cannot step too far beyond the bounds of what we will accept. Their trade lies in articulating a common culture, and we select that which best fits our conceptions and requirements. But, and it must be emphasised, we can only select from what is there. It is in this respect that the media act as a cultural reservoir. Their limitations are also our limitations, and there is a real sense in which something not provided for in a culture becomes unthinkable. Thus, in research, as well as establishing what the media *do* say, we must also ask about what they don't say, about what is simply absent from the reservoir of conceptions they provide. For instance, a great deal can be learned about media representations of women by asking about the many ways in which they are *not* portrayed, itself a reflection of the restrictions on how they actually are portrayed.

Of course all this is extremely general. In exploring a particular topic like alcoholism we would have to begin with a detailed analysis of the media's representation of it so as to establish exactly what it is that our culture takes for granted in this area. Accordingly, it wouldn't make a lot of sense to discuss alcoholism alone. We would need to analyse out the characteristics of the whole range of the presentation of alcohol in movies and television, the pattern within which representations of alcoholism take on their meaning. With that in mind let me complete this highly schematic discussion by suggesting some of the outer limits of that sort of work.

Media treatment of alcohol can be conveniently classified into three areas: alcohol treated as (A) part of the routinised background, (B) part of the routinised foreground, and (C) as exceptional foreground. The line between (B) and (C) may often be blurred (what is considered routine may be rendered exceptional, and vice-versa) but this division has some heuristic value. Let me consider each in turn.

(A) routinised background
Here drinking is presented as a taken-for-granted feature of the world of the film or programme and is not foregrounded in any way. For those still 'learning', such a background offers a setting into which they may be socialised: an image of the character of drinking places, an account of what constitutes appropriate modes of behaviour in such situations, and a range of possible 'styles' of alcohol consumption. A definition, if you like, of drinking normality. Representations of this type—precisely because they are part of the taken-for-granted back-

11

ground—can be far reaching. It is here that we learn the norms of acceptable behaviour in drinking matters. But it doesn't stop there. In adulthood such routinised images confirm the widespread acceptability of the various forms of social drinking. They feature as part of a complex circle of legitimation: we routinely behave in certain ways, and we are able to render that behaviour non-problematic (in the sense that we do not query it) because other people, both in fact and in cultural representation, are routinely behaving similarly. Such constant repetition ensures that drinking remains an un-selfconscious process for us. So the appropriate research questions in this area must focus on precisely what patterns are taken for granted, and how they relate—if they do—to distinct and isolatable audiences. In short, we need to establish and document the media's taken-for-granted ideas about 'normal' drinking.

(B) routinised foreground
It's worth distinguishing two forms here.

(i) non-problematic
In this category fall those cases in which drinking is foregrounded but not in such a way as to make it appear a problem-raising activity. In such instances, almost by default, drinking carries positive connotations: if something is a foreground topic, and yet not problematic, then the very fact of its prominence suggests a positive evaluation. The most common users of such simple stereotyping are alcohol advertisements where drinking is foregrounded into contexts intended to signify goodness, excitement, health, fun, masculinity, or whatever is considered most appropriate for the target social groups. The class and regional variations of beer advertisements, for instance, are rich in techniques for foregrounding drinking in socially appealing ways. But outside of advertisements non-problematic foregrounding is not so common. When drink is prominent in films or TV drama it is generally given some sort of gloss as a problem. Hence a second sub-class:

(ii) semi-problematic
This area probably has the most research potential since it requires us to explore the ways in which the media define the flexible borderline between absolute deviance (generally reserved for alcoholism) and, so to speak, acceptable drunkenness. That isn't to suggest that films or TV programmes act as simple moral arbiters. Rather they give currency to ways of seeing, understanding, even 'doing' drunkenness, ways that are widely articulated throughout our culture. Consider, for example, the case argued by MacAndrew and Edgerton.[10] On the basis of comparative research into drunken comportment, they argue that alcohol, whatever its undeniable physical effects, does not have the same consequences from one culture to another. It is not, as many have argued, a simple disinhibitor. Our behaviour when drunk, like our behaviour when sober, is channelled in socially specific ways. Drunkenness is partly learned; it operates within discoverable limits. As they put it:

Over the course of socialisation, people learn about drunkenness what their society 'knows' about drunkenness; and, accepting and acting upon the understandings thus imparted to them, they become the living confirmation of their society's teachings.[11]

Needless to say, such learning is a complex process. Our images of drunkenness have more than one source, but it is surely inevitable that the media play an important part in this process of collective articulation.

There are, then, two levels in the process of typifying drunkenness. At one level we find models of how one routinely behaves when drunk, models which vary across cultures and within cultures in application to different circumstances. They provide us with the forms in which we cast our drunken behaviour. At a second level different ways of 'being drunk' are associated with different values: lines are drawn between drunkenness as thoroughly deviant, as tolerable, as funny, even as admirable. A central research task would be to identify the varieties of drunkenness represented in the media, the contexts in which they feature, and the degree to which they are designated problematic. Though there may be no single model of drunkenness in a culture, that does not mean that there is no pattern to be discovered. Nor, of course, is drunkenness the only alcohol-related problem area foregrounded in the media, though it is possibly the most common. There are other stereotypes which could profitably be researched in this area.

(C) exceptional foreground

Classically this area covers alcoholism and the alcoholic: the representation of actions and attitudes defined, in the treatment they receive from the media, as Serious Problems. Perhaps the most interesting general questions to ask here revolve around the drawing of a boundary between 'alcoholism' and 'heavy drinking'. For many of us, with necessarily limited experience, our conception of the alcoholic is formed via the stereotypes found in the movies or on TV, stereotypes which change over time and in relation to different social situations. That sort of typification is explored in some detail elsewhere in this book, so I shall not pursue it here. I will only pause to observe that this is a pattern which has to be understood in the framework provided by the media's general treatment of alcohol. It cannot be considered as an isolated feature.

*　　　　　*　　　　　*

I have tried to argue that, for as long as we retain a simple conception of media effects, we will discover only contradictory or inconclusive evidence about the relation between media representations and our social life. The link cannot be construed in straightforward cause/effect terms; people are not as easily manipulated as that. But the repetition of particular stereotypes, specific ways of seeing and comprehending the world, shapes our culture. And the limits of our culture at any time are the limits of our collective understanding. In articulating those limits, the media do have an effect, a cultural effect. To explore it is to explore a complex part of our social life, and it first requires detailed knowledge of the stereotypes, the images, and the stories which are routinised in our cultures. Only with that sort of knowledge can we hope to demystify the workings of our media, and so begin to understand the role they play in forming and reforming the very worlds in which we live.

Notes

[1] Stan Cohen, *Folk Devils and Moral Panics,* London, 1972. The moral panic that interests Cohen here is that surrounding the confrontations between mods and rockers in the mid-sixties.

[2] See, for example, J. T. Klapper, *The Effects of Mass Communication,* New York, 1960; Roger L. Brown, 'Approaches to the Historical Development of Mass Media Studies' in Jeremy Tunstall (ed.), *Media Sociology,* London 1970; Denis McQuail, 'The Influence and Effects of Mass Media' in James Curran, Michael Gurevitch and Janet Woollacott (eds.), *Mass Communication and Society,* London, 1977. And many others.

[3] Many volumes of the Payne Fund Studies have now been reprinted by the Arno Press of New York. Perhaps the most interesting is the volume by Herbert Blumer, *Movies and Conduct,* New York, 1935.

[4] C. Wright Mills, *The Power Elite,* New York, 1959, p. 314.

[5] The best known of the work on propaganda was probably that conducted in the American Soldier researches and reported in Carl Hovland, Arthur Lumsdaine and Fred D. Sheffield, *Experiments in Mass Communications,* New York, 1949. But there was also a great deal of less well known work.

[6] The responsibility for this 'rediscovery of the primary group' is usually attributed to Elihu Katz and Paul F. Lazarsfeld in their study *Personal Influence,* Glencoe (Ill.), 1955.

[7] J. T. Klapper, *The Effects of Mass Communication,* op. cit.

[8] For an excellent short summary of work in this area see André Glucksmann, *Violence on the Screen,* London, 1971.

[9] These terms owe something to the work of Peter Berger. Especially Peter Berger and Thomas Luckmann, *The Social Construction of Reality,* Harmondsworth, 1967, and Peter Berger, *The Sacred Canopy,* New York, 1967. However, I do not intend them to carry the whole apparatus of Berger's style of work.

[10] Craig MacAndrew and Robert B. Edgerton, *Drunken Comportment,* London, 1970.

[11] *ibid,* p. 88.

The Role of Stereotypes

by Richard Dyer

The word 'stereotype' is today almost always a term of abuse. This stems from the wholly justified objections of various groups—in recent years, blacks, women and gays, in particular[1] —to the ways in which they find themselves stereotyped in the mass media and in everyday speech. Yet when Walter Lippmann coined the term, he did not intend it to have a wholly and necessarily pejorative connotation. Taking a certain ironic distance on his subject, Lippman nonetheless lays out very clearly both the absolute necessity for, and usefulness of, stereotypes, as well as their limitations and ideological implications:

> A pattern of stereotypes is not neutral. It is not merely a way of substituting order for the great blooming, buzzing confusion of reality. It is not merely a short cut. It is all these things and something more. It is the guarantee of our self-respect; it is the projection upon the world of our own sense of our own value, our own position and our own rights. The stereotypes are, therefore, highly charged with the feelings that are attached to them. They are the fortress of our tradition, and behind its defenses we can continue to feel ourselves safe in the position we occupy.[2]

We can begin to understand something of how stereotypes work by following up the ideas raised by Lippmann—in particular his stress on stereotypes as (i) an ordering process, (ii) a 'short cut', (iii) referring to 'the world', and (iv) expressing 'our' values and beliefs. The rest of this essay is structured around these topics, concluding with some tentative remarks on the relevance of what has gone before to the representation of alcoholism. Throughout, I move between the more sociological concern of Lippmann (how stereotypes function in social thought) and the specific aesthetic concerns (how stereotypes function in fictions) that must also be introduced into any consideration of media representations. The position behind all these considerations is that it is not stereotypes, as an aspect of human thought and representation, that are wrong, but who controls and defines them, what interests they serve.

(i) Stereotypes as a form of 'ordering' the mass of complex and inchoate data that we receive from the world are only a particular form—to do with the representation and categorisation of persons[3] —of the wider process by which any human society, and individuals within it, make sense of that society through generalities, patternings and 'typifications'. Unless one believes that there is some definitively 'true' order in the world which is transparently revealed to human beings and unproblematically expressed in their culture—a belief that the variety of orders proposed by different societies, as analysed by anthropology and history, makes difficult to sustain—this activity of ordering, including the use of stereotypes, has to be acknowledged as a necessary, indeed

15

inescapable, part of the way societies make sense of themselves, and hence actually make and reproduce themselves. (The fact that all such orderings are, by definition, partial and limited does not mean that they are untrue—partial knowledge is not false knowledge, it is simply not absolute knowledge.)

There are, however, two problems about stereotypes within this perspective. Firstly, the need to order 'the great blooming, buzzing confusion of reality' is liable to be accompanied by a belief in the absoluteness and certainty of any particular order, a refusal to recognise its limitations and partiality, its relativity and changeability, and a corresponding incapacity to deal with the fact and experience of blooming and buzzing.

Secondly, as the work of Peter Berger and Thomas Luckmann, amongst others, on the 'social construction of reality' stresses, not only is any given society's ordering of reality an historical product, but it is also necessarily implicated in the power relations in that society—as Berger and Luckmann put it, 'he who has the bigger stick has the better chance of imposing his definitions of reality.'[4] I shall return below to these two problems of Lippmann's formulation—order (stereotypes) perceived as absolute and rigid, order (stereotypes) as grounded in social power.

(ii) Lippmann's notion of stereotypes as a short cut points to the manner in which stereotypes are a very simple, striking, easily-grasped form of representation but are nonetheless capable of condensing a great deal of complex information and a host of connotations. As T. E. Perkins notes in her key article 'Rethinking Stereotypes', the often observed 'simplicity' of stereotypes is deceptive:

. . . to refer 'correctly' to someone as a 'dumb blonde', and to understand what is meant by that implies a great deal more than hair colour and intelligence. It refers immediately to *her* sex, which refers to her status in society, her relationship to men, her inability to behave or think rationally, and so on. In short, it implies knowledge of a complex social structure. . . .[5]

The same point emerges from Arnold S. Linsky's analysis of the representation of the alcoholic in popular magazines between 1900 and 1966, where changing depictions of alcoholics are shown to express complex and contradictory social theories, not merely of alcoholism but of free will and determinism.[6]

(iii) Lippmann refers to stereotypes as a projection on to the 'world'. Although he is not primarily concerned to distinguish stereotypes from modes of representation whose principal concern is not the world, it is important for us to do so, especially as our focus is representations in media *fictions,* which are aesthetic and well as social constructs. In this perspective, stereotypes are a particular sub-category of a broader category of fictional characters, the type. Whereas stereotypes are essentially defined, as in Lippmann, by their social function, types, at this level of generality, are primarily defined by their aesthetic function, namely, as a mode of characterisation in fiction. The type is any character constructed through the use of a few immediately recognisable and defining traits, that do not change or 'develop' through the course of the narrative and which point to general, recurrent features of the human world (whether these features are conceptualised as universal and eternal, the 'archetype', or historically and culturally specific, 'social types' and 'stereotypes'—a distinction discussed below).[7] The opposite of the type is the novelistic character, defined by a multiplicity of traits that are only gradually revealed to us through the course of the narrative, a narrative which is hinged on the growth or development of the character and is thus centred upon the latter in her or his unique individuality, rather than pointing outwards to a world.

In our society, it is the novelistic character that is privileged over the type,[8] for the obvious reason that our society privileges—at any rate, at the level of social rhetoric—the individual over the collective or the mass. For this reason, the majority of fictions that address themselves to general social issues tend nevertheless to end up telling the story of a particular individual, hence returning social issues to purely personal and psychological ones. Once we address ourselves to the representation and definition of social categories—e.g. alcoholics—we have to consider what is at stake in one mode of characterisation rather than another. Where do we want the emphasis of the representation to lie—on the psychological (alcoholism as a personal problem), on the social (alcoholism as an aspect of society) or in some articulation of the two? The choice or advocacy of a more novelistic or a more typical representation implicitly expresses one or other of these emphases.[9]

(iv) It is Lippmann's reference to *our* tradition, and indeed his use of 'our' and 'we' throughout the passage quoted, that takes us into the most important, and most problematic, issue in stereotyping. For we have to ask, who exactly is the 'we' and 'us' invoked by Lippmann?—is it necessarily you and me?

The effectiveness of stereotypes resides in the way they invoke a consensus. Stereotypes proclaim, 'This is what everyone—you, me and us—thinks members of such-and-such a social group are like', as if these concepts of these social groups were spontaneously arrived at by all members of society independently and in isolation. The stereotype is taken to express a general agreement about a social group, as if that agreement arose before, and independently of, the stereotype. Yet for the most part it is *from* stereotypes that we get our ideas about social groups. The consensus invoked by stereotypes is more apparent than real; rather, stereotypes express particular definitions of reality, with concomitant evaluations, which in turn relate to the disposition of power within society. Who proposes the stereotype, who has the power to enforce it, is the crux of the matter—*whose* tradition is Lippmann's 'our tradition'?

Here Orrin E. Klapp's distinction between stereotypes and social types is helpful. In his book, *Heroes, Villains and Fools*,[10] Klapp defines social types as representations of those who 'belong' to society. They are the kinds of people that one expects, and is led to expect, to find in one's society, whereas stereotypes are those who do not belong, who are outside of one's society. In Klapp, this distinction is principally geographic—i.e. social types of Americans, stereotypes of non-Americans. We can, however, rework his distinction in terms of the types produced by different social groups according to their sense of who belongs and who doesn't, who is 'in' and who is not. Who does or does not belong to a given society as a whole is then a function of the relative power of groups in that society to define themselves as central and the rest as 'other', peripheral or outcast.

In fictions, social types and stereotypes can be recognised as distinct by the different ways in which they can be used. Social types, although constructed inconographically similarly to the way stereotypes are constructed (i.e. the way a few verbal and visual traits are used to signal the character), can be used in a much more open and flexible way than can stereotypes. This is most clearly seen in relation to plot. Social types can figure in almost any kind of plot and can have a wide range of roles in that plot (e.g. as hero, as villain, as helper, as light relief, etc.), whereas stereotypes always carry within their very representation an implicit narrative. Jo Spence has argued in the context of the representation of women that despite the superficial variety of images, they all carry within them an implicit narrative pattern:

> . . . visual representations which may appear to deal with diverse ideas but which are all aimed at women tend to act as part of an implicit narrative. This has a 'beginning' and a 'middle' (birth, childhood, marriage, family life) but there is only minimal representation of its 'end', of growing old and dying.[11]

In an article dealing with the stereotyping of gays in films, I tried to show how the use of images of lesbians in a group of French films, no matter what kind of film or of what 'artistic quality', always involved an identical plot function.[12] Similarly, we surely only have to be told that we are going to see a film about an alcoholic to know that it will be a tale either of sordid decline or of inspiring redemption. (This suggests a particularly interesting use of stereotypes, in which the character is constructed, at the level of dress, performance, etc., as a stereotype but is deliberately given a narrative function that is not implicit in the stereotype, thus throwing into question the assumptions signalled by the stereotypical iconography.)

The social type/stereotype distinction is essentially one of degree. It is after all very hard to draw a line between those who are just within and those definitely beyond the pale. This is partly because different social categories overlap—e.g. men 'belong', blacks do not, but what of black men? It is also because some of the categories that the social type/stereotype distinction keeps apart cannot logically be kept apart in this way. The obvious examples here are men and women, and it is this that causes T. E. Perkins to reject the distinction.[13] As applied to men and women, the social type/stereotype distinction implies that men have no direct experience of women and that there could be a society composed entirely of men: both of these are virtually impossible.

Yet it seems to me that what the distinction points to, as applied to women and men, is a tendency of patriarchal thought[14] to attempt to maintain the impossible, by insisting on the 'otherness' of women and men (or rather the 'otherness' of women, men being in patriarchy the human norm to which women are 'other') in the face of their necessary collaboration in history and society. (The distinction does also refer in part to a real separation in social arrangements, i.e. the fact of male and female 'preserves': the pub, the beauty salon, the study, the kitchen, etc.). What the distinction also maintains is the *absolute* difference between men and women, in the face of their actual relative similarity.[15]

This is the most important function of the stereotype, to maintain sharp boundary definitions, to define clearly where the pale ends and thus who is clearly within and who clearly beyond it. Stereotypes do not only, in concert with social types, map out the boundaries of acceptable and legitimate behaviour, they also insist on boundaries exactly at those points where in reality there are none. Nowhere is this more clear than with stereotypes dealing with social categories that are invisible and/or fluid. Such categories are *invisible,* because you cannot tell just from looking at a person that she or he belongs to the category in question. Unless the person chooses to dress or act in a clearly and culturally defined manner (e.g. the working class man's cloth cap, the male homosexual's limp wrist) or unless one has a trained eye (as those dealing with alcoholics have?), it is impossible to place the person before one, whereas many social groups—women and men, different races, young and old—are visibly different, and this difference can only be eradicated by disguise. Social categories can be *fluid,* in the sense that it is not possible in reality to draw a line between them and adjacent categories. We make a fuss about—and produce stereotypes about—the difference between women and men, yet biologically this is negligible compared to their similarity. Again, we are led to treat heterosexuality and homosexuality as sharply opposed categories of persons when in reality both heterosexual and homosexual responses and behaviour are to some extent experienced by everybody in their life. Alcohol use is clearly in this category—it is notoriously difficult to draw the line between harm-free and harmful drinking. But stereotypes can.

The role of stereotypes is to make visible the invisible, so that there is no danger of it creeping on us unawares; and to make fast, firm and separate what is in reality fluid and much closer to the norm than the dominant value system cares to admit.

In the widest sense, these functions of rendering visible and firm can be connected to Lippmann's insistence on stereotypes as ordering concepts, and to the tendency towards rigidity that may be implied by this. All societies need to have relatively stable boundaries and categories, but this stability can be achieved within a context that recognises the relativity and uncertainty of concepts. Such a stability is, however, only achieved in a situation of real, as opposed to imposed, consensus. The degree of rigidity and shrillness of a stereotype indicates the degree to which it is an enforced representation that points to a reality whose invisibility and/or fluidity threatens the received definitions of society promoted by those with the biggest sticks. (E.g. if women are not so very different from men, why are they subordinated?; if alcoholism is not so easily distinguished from social drinking, can we be so comfortable in our acceptance of the latter and condemnation of the former?)

In this perspective, and speaking very tentatively, what is striking about the current media representation of alcoholism is its absence. It seems no longer to be identified as a key social personal problem, to be marked stereotypically as beyond the pale of 'normal' behaviour. Rather it hardly seems to be there at all. This may be related to the development of marijuana use as a focus of media/'public' concern—dope addicts are among the most shrill of today's stereotypes. In this context, all alcohol use seems redolent of old-fashioned values, and especially of 'masculine' values set against the 'effeminacy' of 'hippie' culture. To this one would add the enormous financial involvement of the alcohol industry in the leisure industries, of which the media are a key part, and in particular the reliance of television and cinema on advertising revenue (which, in the current legal situation, cannot come from marijuana promotion but can, and does, from alcohol promotion).

If we look back at the cinema, however, it is fairly clear that the alcoholic did serve *to distinguish clearly* alcohol use from abuse, as if a definite line could be drawn, in order to legitimate the 'social' use of alcohol. This includes the legitimation of excessive consumption, drunkenness and other alcohol-induced anti-social behaviour, since it is possible, by the use of stereotypes, to see this as distinct from 'real' alcoholism. The question that such an analysis poses is, in whose interest was this distinction maintained?[16]

Notes

[1] In relation to film, see Jim Pines, *Blacks and Films* (Studio Vista, London, 1975), Claire Johnston (ed.), *Notes on Women's Cinema* (SEFT, London, 1973), Richard Dyer (ed.), *Gays and Film* (BFI, London, 1977), *inter alia*.

[2] Walter Lippmann, *Public Opinion,* Macmillan, New York, 1956, p. 96. (First published 1922.)

[3] I confine myself here to the discussion of stereotypes as a form of representing persons, although the word itself (especially in adjectival form) is also used to refer to ideas, behaviour, settings, etc.

[4] Peter Berger and Thomas Luckmann, *The Social Construction of Reality,* Allen Lane, Penguin Press, 1967, p. 127. It should be pointed out that Berger and Luckmann do not follow up this question of power as insistently as they might.

[5] T. E. Perkins, 'Rethinking Stereotypes' in Michele Barrett, Phil Corrigan, Annette Kuhn and Janet Wolfe (eds.), *Ideology and Cultural Production.* Croom Helm, New York, 1979, p. 139.

[6] Arnold S. Linsky, 'Theories of behaviour and the image of the alcoholic in popular magazines 1900–1966', *Public Opinion Quarterly* 34, Winter 1970–71, pp. 573–81.

[7] It is important to stress the role of conceptualisation in the distinction between, on the one hand, archetypes, and on the other, social and stereotypes, since what may be attributed to a type as a universal and eternal trait, hence making it archetypal, may only be a historically and culturally specific trait misunderstood as a universal and eternal trait—it is, after all, the tendency of dominant value systems in societies to pass their values off as universally and eternally valid.

[8] See Ian Watt, *The Rise of the Novel* (Penguin 1963) for a discussion of the specificity of such characterisation to the novel form and hence to modern capitalist societies. The distinction between type and novelistic character is discussed in *The Dumb Blonde Stereotype*, BFI Educational Advisory Service, 1979.

[9] Among the approaches to this problem that may be signalled here are those of Lukacs, Brecht, Eisenstein and Claire Johnston and Pam Cook.

[10] Orrin E. Klapp, *Heroes, Villains and Fools*, Prentice-Hall, Engelwood Cliffs, 1962.

[11] Jo Spence, 'What do people do all day? Class and Gender in Images of Women', *Screen Education* 29.

[12] *Gays and Film*, pp. 33–35.

[13] See Perkins, op.cit., pp. 140–1.

[14] By patriarchy I mean the thought system that legitimates the power of men and the subordination of women in society; I do not mean that it is necessarily and simply how all men think of women, although it is an overwhelming determinant on that.

[15] See Ann Oakley, *Sex, Gender and Society*, Temple Smith, London, 1972.

[16] It is interesting to note that the liquor industry has been anxious to reinforce the view that alcoholism is a special disease suffered by a minority of the population, rather than varieties of harm, which anyone might experience in varying degrees, simply as a result of drinking too much too often. A preventive policy based upon the latter view might well be aimed at reducing levels of consumption (and hence revenue) whereas this would be quite inappropriate in terms of the former view.

Part Two: Alcoholism in the Movies

An Overview

by Mike Lewington

The way in which alcoholism as a phenomenon has been conceptualised in this century has undergone a number of significant changes. This sequence of transformations has been referred to by Gusfield as a 'moral passage'.[1] The four models of alcoholism that have thus obtained are detailed below.

These shifts were not abrupt, in the sense that everyone at some point ceased believing in one model and subscribed to another. Moreover some groups maintained and still maintain adherence to a previous model. It was rather the case that society invests different groups at different times with the responsibility for defining and ameliorating certain social problems and that these groups necessarily evolve ways of understanding and managing the problems which legitimise their ownership of them.

The Moral Model
A model in which alcoholism is not perceived as a discrete condition or syndrome in the medical sense, but rather as an indulgence in persistent excessive drinking, usually typified as 'drunkenness', in itself an immoral activity, and resulting in a dereliction of responsibility in the home and in the workplace. Drunkenness is seen as being the result of a moral flaw or spiritual degeneracy. Responsibility for arresting and ameliorating the condition would be located in religious or quasi-religious institutions and entail spiritual and moral guidance leading to a successful outcome defined in terms of the resumption of familial duties, church attendance and abstinence.

Two views about the aetiology of drunkenness common at the time and not mutually exclusive were: that there was a daemonic quality to the substance alcohol (the Demon Drink) such that of itself it was inherently evil, and secondly that there were groups in society that were responsible for spreading the moral contagion by the seduction of those vulnerable to temptation through moral weakness.[2]

For those subscribing to this model, preventive initiatives would logically be focused on the restriction of the availability of alcohol, confinement of contagious groups, and the maintenance of high levels of moral rectitude in society.

The Biological or Disease Model
By the mid-thirties the idea that alcoholism was, in some sense, a disease had

steadily gained ground. This model was popularised by the foundation and growth of Alcoholics Anonymous, whose orthodoxy states that alcoholism is 'an allergy of the body and an obsession of the mind'. Those espousing this view assumed that alcoholics were genetically different from other people such that their relationship with alcohol would entail an inevitable progression of increased consumption leading to death unless treatment was sought.[3] Attempts to isolate the differentiating factor proved inconclusive; nevertheless the disease model proved popular for a number of reasons. At a pragmatic level, it appears to be the case that funding for research and the establishment of facilities is more forthcoming for physiological rather than spiritual maladies. Moreover the typification of a phenomenon as a disease rather than a moral flaw reduces the level of stigma by the implication that alcoholics are not responsible for their condition. It may well be for these reasons, rather than concern for intellectual rigour, that this model was taken up so readily.

There are, however, a number of implications inherent within this model. The first is that alcoholism is genetically determined, rather than being the result of drinking too much too often. The second is that the appropriate locus for treatment is medical and that diagnosis of the condition depends upon the exhibition of detectable symptoms: e.g. delerium tremens, craving, dependence, hallucinations. This effectively precludes early recognition, a problem further exacerbated by the contemporary belief that the alcoholic had to hit 'rock bottom' before becoming amenable to treatment. The third implication is that successful treatment will be defined in terms of abstinence, and fourthly, that in any meaningful sense prevention of the condition over a whole population was not feasible except presumably by some form of screening at birth should a differentiating factor be identified.

The Psychological Model

With the expansion in the 1940s and 1950s of psychoanalysis as a body of theory and practice, a model of alcoholism began to emerge derived from psychoanalytic and particularly Freudian theory. This model espoused the view that alcoholism, still perceived as a discrete condition, resulted from unresolved traumatic childhood experiences. A view popular at the time was that alcoholism was caused by fixation in the oral mode, or more specifically was a sublimation of latent homosexuality.[4]

Within this model treatment would appropriately be located within the psychiatric services and take the form of depth analysis. As with the disease model, this model effectively precludes prevention and early recognition by utilising a definition of alcoholism which entails significant damage as a credential for entry into treatment services.

The Sociological Model

In the 1950s work was carried out which identified striking differences in rates of alcoholism between different cultural groups in an American city; the Jewish and Irish communities were found to have disproportionally low and high rates respectively.[5] This led to the formulation of a view that the rates of alcoholism within a particular culture were a factor of that culture's attitude towards drinking. Since that time work has continued on identifying a range of factors which would contribute to placing someone in a high risk position: e.g. locality, sex, age, occupation.

Moreover the view that alcoholics are in some way psychologically or biologically different from other people began to be challenged, and a view evolved that anyone who drank sufficient quantities over a sufficient period could achieve dependence, and furthermore, that the rate of problems within a given population was related to the per capita consumption of that population.[6]

Parallel with these developments, the concept of alcoholism as a discrete condition was eroded and the term applied more generally to cover anyone experiencing problems of a physical, psychological or social nature as a result of their drinking.[7]

This model might be summarised as regarding alcoholism as an individual's response to a range of external factors. This model has no specific implications for treatment of the individual, but does provide scope for early recognition, both by the identification of high risk factors, and a broader definition of what constitutes alcoholism; and prevention of alcoholism through the manipulation of levels of consumption by fiscal means or other limitations of availability or through changing cultural attitudes through programmes of health education is operationally valid.

It seems to be the case that for a range of problems the clergy, doctors, psychiatrists and sociologists have each in turn assumed responsibility and that this sequence may in turn be a manifestation of a more general transformation in the way in which we view the relationship between the individual and society. In other words, we have moved in the last hundred years from a position in which humanity is seen as being essentially free and responsible for its predicament to a position in which its predicament is seen as being determined by external factors.[8]

Whether these shifts have entered the consciousness of the public at large has been investigated by Linsky[9] in his analysis of the theories of behaviour and causation in popular magazine articles on alcoholism. He argues that such magazines depend upon wide reader acceptance and thus would tend to reflect or be at the most slightly in advance of contemporary public opinion. His research, which covered the period 1900–1966, established that a shift from a moral model to a biological/psychological model had occurred by 1940 and that although this model still predominates in this medium, there has been a continuing trend towards sociological explanations.

The questions that this chapter seeks to address are: to what extent does the representation of alcoholism in the cinema reflect contemporary models; and secondly, within the range of possible modes of representation, which particular aspects of the phenomenon have been selected as representative of an alcoholic career?

A film, in view of its structure and content being determined by other forces than the primary need to present a coherent set of concepts, may borrow ideas from diverse models, resulting in inconsistency at an intellectual level, or use different models at different levels of meaning, or, in the case of more than one alcoholic being present in any one film, a different model for each. Alcoholism is by no means unique in this respect.

Considering the moral model first, it is clear that the films of the thirties conformed to the contemporary orthodoxy. Such films as *What Price Hollywood* (1932) and *Vessel of Wrath* (1938) do not seek to differentiate the drinker as essentially different from other men. In the former, which takes a critical view of Hollywood mores, the drinker's repugnance at his condition eventually leads to suicide, whilst in the latter he is reformed through contact with a missionary whom he in turn humanises.

This model is perpetuated into the forties, as is evidenced by *Key Largo* (1948), in which the condition of an alcoholic gangster's moll, Gaye Dawn (Claire Trevor), is seen as stemming from her involvement with a morally corrupt group of gangsters led by Johnny Rocco, whose extreme moral degeneracy is symbolised by drinking whisky whilst bathing. She achieves redemption by an act of personal courage in which she transfers her allegiance from the gangsters to the Bogart-Bacall faction.

The theme of redemption through an act of courage similarly typifies the termination of the alcoholic career of major characters in *Rio Bravo* (1959) and *The Squeeze* (1977). In the former film, a western, Dude (Dean Martin), whose alcoholism has been caused by his girlfriend's desertion, recovers not only by modelling on John Wayne, whose behaviour regarding both women and alcohol is moderate, but also by taking the opportunity to risk his life in the upholding of law and order. This film was remade as *El Dorado* in 1967 and the alcoholism theme diminished in significance through the introduction of a miracle cure administered by Mississippi (James Caan). In *The Squeeze* (1977), a Sweeneyesque detective story set in contemporary London, the hero achieves sobriety and regains his self-respect through saving his kidnapped daughter. In the film the hero is detoxified in hospital and given a form of aversion therapy but this is demonstrably ineffective and irrelevant to the main business of the film.

Interestingly the biological model informs few films in its pure form. It is most evident in *Come Back Little Sheba* (1952) in which Alcoholics Anonymous figures significantly both in ideological and plot terms, appearing as a flying squad ready to intervene when Doc (Burt Lancaster) periodically relapses, to ferry him off to hospital for compulsory detoxification. Whilst all the characters subscribe to and articulate a view of alcoholism as an unchangeable condition that is ever present and avoided only by abstinence, the underlying meaning of Doc's alcoholism is a rejection of and escape from the monotonous existence that his forced marriage to a pathetic slattern wife has condemned him.

Come Fill the Cup (1951) includes two alcoholics, of which only one conforms to a disease model (James Cagney). Cagney's alcoholism just happens,

25

quickly leading to a loss of job and destitution on skid row. Whilst recovering in hospital from a road accident he is informed of the progressive nature of his condition, the poor prognosis and his difference from other men with regard to alcohol. Surprisingly, the other alcoholic in the film clearly derives his condition from a florid Oedipus complex, and thus demonstrates an opposing model.

Of the films viewed in our season at the NFT the psychological model was predominant either as implicit and vague, as in the case of *The Lost Weekend* (1945), or more explicitly with lavish doses of Hollywood Freud as in *Too Much Too Soon* (1958) or *Days of Wine and Roses* (1962).

Impotence, in terms of sexuality or work, figures as cause or metaphor in *The Lost Weekend, Come Fill the Cup* and *Written on the Wind* (1956). More specific diagnoses are offered in *Come Fill the Cup* and *I'll Cry Tomorrow* (1955)—domination by or fixation upon the mother, whilst the women alcoholics in *Too Much Too Soon* and *Days of Wine and Roses* exhibit sexual attraction towards their fathers and a prodromal obsession with sex and chocolate respectively.

A most subversive film in this respect is *Harvey* (1950), which opposes the warm and accepting behaviour of the alcoholic character (James Stewart) with the artifice, deviousness and inhumanity of the sober world. When told that he must come to terms with reality, he replies that he struggled with reality for thirty years—and finally won. The psychiatrists in the film who utilise both analytical and chemotherapeutic approaches are rendered helpless by the magic at his disposal.

The sociological model was perceptible in one film only of those viewed: *Days of Wine and Roses.* Joe Clay's alcoholism seems to stem from the stressful nature of his job in public relations, compared to the psychological explanation advanced for that of his wife. However, during the course of the film he comes into contact with AA and achieves sobriety through acceptance and enactment of their doctrine. Interestingly one of the AA members commenting on himself states that he is just someone who drank too much too often, a view congruent with present thinking but an anathema to the disease model that AA espouses.

The films viewed can be divided as follows:

Moral	Biological
1932 *What Price Hollywood*	1951 *Come Fill the Cup*
1938 *Vessel of Wrath*	1952 *Come Back Little Sheba*
1948 *Key Largo*	
1954 *A Star is Born*	
1959 *Rio Bravo*	
1967 *El Dorado*	
1977 *The Squeeze**	

*Although the question of aetiology is not explored in the film, there are traces of the myth that policemen are driven to alcoholism by the stressful nature of their work, a theme utilised in *Hazell* (see below).

26

Psychological	_Sociological_
1945 _The Lost Weekend_	1962 _Days of Wine and Roses_
1947 _Smash Up_	
1950 _Harvey_	
1951 _Come Fill the Cup_	
1955 _I'll Cry Tomorrow_	
1956 _Written on the Wind_	
1957 _The Buster Keaton Story_	
1958 _Too Much Too Soon_	
1962 _Days of Wine and Roses_	

It is apparent that the psychological and moral models are prevalent in the films viewed. One reason for this might be that diseases are in a sense too realistic in that they simply 'happen' to one and secondly that there are problems in the representation of social forces in a tradition that focuses on individual characterisation. It is also true that the majority of the films viewed were produced in the fifties at a time in which Hollywood was turning its attention to a range of social problems and reflecting and reinforcing interest in psychoanalytic theory.[10]

Having discussed the parameters in which the particular representations are located, I should now like to focus on those specific aspects of the alcoholic career that have been utilised in the films. These recurring aspects fall into four categories: the fall from wealth to poverty, relapsing, withdrawal, and treatment.

i) The fall from wealth to poverty occurs in most films, the latter often being expressed in terms of hitting skid row, which provides a striking visual analogy to the progression of the condition. Skid row in the films usually entails a decline in dress and personal hygiene and a rise in offensive drunken behaviour sometimes leading to incarceration. It is not usually represented in terms of membership of a sub-culture, indeed the appearance of other skid row characters in an alcoholism movie is rare. One interesting exception to this is _The Squeeze,_ in which the hero's position in relation to skid row is highly ambivalent. Although having a home, children and a strong informal support system, the occasion of his first and only major relapse finds him in the midst of a bottle gang on a building site. This may stem from a belief on the part of the film makers that alcoholism and skid row are synonymous, a confusion that was also evident in the erroneous titling of _Edna the Inebriate Woman,_ the eponymous heroine of which demonstrated little if any evidence of alcohol dependence, or even persistent drunkenness.

Other related elements of decline commonly focused on are loss of job and a breakdown in relations with spouse or lover; the adage that work is the curse of the drinking classes certainly holds in alcoholism movies.[11] The represented effect of alcoholism in relationships is such that it leads men to commit acts of aggression and women to commit acts of promiscuity. (A discussion of the particular elements specific to the representation of women alcoholics is found

27

elsewhere in this book.)

The dramatic potential of the relapse is often fully exploited in those movies in which the alcoholic achieves a period of sobriety, the dramatic interest residing in the question whether or not they can withstand the variety of pressures exerted upon them without resuming drinking.

The continuous threat that alcohol poses to sobriety is often symbolised by a bottle kept in a cupboard, which serves either to remind the owner of the depths from which they have managed to escape, or to provide refreshment for visitors.

ii) The relapse usually entails a loss of control over drinking and usually leads to a misfortune or to some form of compulsory, punitive treatment. The resumption of controlled drinking, an idea which would reduce the dramatic simplicity of the alcoholic/abstainer opposition, is found only in *Rio Bravo*. However, in terms of the Western genre, the teetotal cowboy exists only as a figure of fun, e.g. *The Paleface* (1948).

iii) Withdrawal symptoms figure in most alcoholism movies, only occasionally being replaced by a significant, i.e. change-inducing, misfortune, for example in *Smash Up* (1947), where Angel (Susan Hayward) sets fire to her room and almost incinerates herself and her child. In fact women alcoholics tend not to exhibit violent withdrawal, the exception being Lillian Roth (Susan Hayward) in *I'll Cry Tomorrow*. *The Lost Weekend* offered a mode of representation that was readily adopted by later movies; Don Birnam exhibits craving, tremor, sweating, delirium tremens and hallucinations. Other characters in the 'drunk tank' scene exhibit, or are reported to exhibit, horrifying symptoms of a similar nature. After a brief period of popularity hallucinations had all but disappeared by 1951, possibly due to the stylistic difficulties inherent in their representations within a tradition of realism. Delirium tremens continued as the most common signifying symptom, reaching its most dramatic though not realistic realisation in *Days of Wine and Roses,* complete with straight jacket and padded cell.

iv) Modes of treatment represented can be divided into two aspects; formal and informal. Formal treatment throughout the films is represented as at least custodial, if not punitive, the image of the locked door or barred window being a common feature. A sadistic or pessimistic male nurse or custodian is a regular motif, and often other patients exhibit frightening behaviour. Treatment within institutions is usually unsuccessful; the only alternative presented within the movies is AA, which is always typified as effective often through the personal relationships developed therein rather than through an engagement in the formal processes as such. One aspect of AA's approach that is always represented or reported, usually the former, is the public definition of oneself as an alcoholic at an AA meeting. This signifies in terms of the films that abstinence is imminent, and of itself is regarded as an act of courage. Informal treatment, either through the curative power of an intimate relationship, or engaging in acts of courage leading to an improved self-esteem, is represented as the most effective kind. The idea of autobiography as a therapeutic endeavour is found in three films: *The Lost Weekend, I''ll Cry Tomorrow* and *Too Much Too Soon,* and is congruent with the psychological model that informs them. (Discussion of the representation of treatment is expanded by Bruce Ritson— see below.)

The types of people who engage in these careers are not drawn from a very wide spectrum of society. In the films viewed, most were in their thirties and were comfortably well off, if not actually wealthy, prior to the onset of the condition; one can see how this might be functional in emphasising the fall to skid row. As regards professions, half the alcoholics represented were in the entertainment industry, primarily in films, but also in cabaret, writing and musical composition. Most of the professions were, or were represented as being, individualistic rather than cooperative.

To summarise, it would seem that the models which predominantly inform the films are moral and psychological, but that the focus of interest in most films is biologically orientated: withdrawal symptoms, progressivity of the condition entailing relapse, and abstinence as the only goal. In spite of the emphasis on a psychological aetiology, psychiatric services are represented as at best inept and at worst punitive. No other services are represented, apart from AA which appears to corner the market, at least in organisational terms, as far as effective treatment is concerned, although stress is laid on the curative power of close relationships. The alcoholic career is typified by violent symptoms and hitting rock bottom often involving skid row, and those likely to engage in this career are well-off, middle-class people, usually male, employed in a creative profession.

Notes

[1] Joseph Gusfield, 'Moral Passage: The Symbolic Process in Public Designations of Deviance', *Social Problems,* Fall 1967, pp. 175–188.

[2] See Joseph Gusfield, *Symbolic Crusade: Status Politics and the American Temperance Movement,* University of Illinois, Urbana, 1963.

[3] David Robinson, *Talking Out of Alcoholism: The Self-Help Process of Alcoholics Anonymous,* Croom Helm, 1979, contains a concise account of the development of AA and its current practice. Robinson points out that comparatively little attention is given to aetiological factors as opposed to procedures for recovery within that organisation.

[4] See Earl Small and B. Leach, 'Counselling Homosexual Alcoholics', *Journal of Studies on Alcohol,* v. 38, n. 11, 1977, pp. 2077–2086.

[5] E.g. R. F. Bales, 'Cultural Differences in Rates of Alcoholism', *Quarterly Journal of Studies on Alcoholism,* 6, 1946, pp. 480–499.

[6] See D. L. Davies (ed.), *The Ledermann Curve,* Alcohol Education Centre, 1977.

[7] See D. L. Davies, *Implications for Medical Practice of an Acceptable Concept of Alcoholism,* Alcohol Education Centre, 1977.

[8] Arnold Linsky, 'Theories of Behaviour and the Image of the Alcoholic in Popular Magazines 1900–1966', *Public Opinion Quarterly,* 34, Winter 1970–71.

[9] Linsky, op cit.

[10] See Parker Tyler, *Magic and Myth of the Movies,* Henry Holt & Co. Ltd., 1947.

[11] See Eric Berne, *What Do You Say After You Say Hello?,* Andre Deutsch, 1974, p. 103, and more generally Claude Steiner, *Scripts People Live,* Grove Press Inc., 1974, for an exploration of this opposition.

The Alcoholic as Hero

by Marcus Grant

The hero (or, indeed, the heroine) who is portrayed as an alcoholic is of particular interest both from a dramatic and thematic point of view. Alcoholism provides great potential for the development of a range of dramatic situations whilst at the same time creating a credible and readily comprehensible tragic flaw.

It is the ambivalence of dominant but not necessarily consonant notions of alcoholism which make it such an interesting condition to visit upon a hero. On the one hand, it is a self-inflicted condition, since people do not become alcoholics unless they choose to drink prodigious quantities of alcohol. A question which remains unanswered is why it is that they should choose to drink so much that they become alcoholics at all. Since most films espouse aetiological models relying upon biological or psychoanalytic explanations, it can be seen that there is a kind of shabby determinism at work here. Thus, despite the fact that alcoholics are, on one level, free to drink or not to drink, this freedom is shown as illusory, since alcoholism has an air of inexorable progression so that, particularly with the concept of alcoholism that has predominated in the movies, it takes the hero into deeper and deeper suffering before, if ever, releasing him. Thus, the choice, *however made,* to drink excessively, for whatever reason, is generally made *without* a desire to embrace the consequences of that choice. But a hero is expected to be held responsible for the consequences of his choices, even when these consequences are unforeseen. It both is, and is not, his fault that he becomes an alcoholic, in rather the same way that it both is, and is not, the fault of Oedipus that he murders his father and marries his mother. Alcoholism becomes a metaphor for destiny.

Since the concern of this book is with dramatic representations of alcoholism, it is worth considering three rather different images which have tended to be presented on the screen. These images have very different implications even though they do, in reality, form a continuum of drinking styles; their dramatic potential depends upon the point on the continuum where the individual is located.

Firstly, the image of *the drinker* is clearly an attractive one, carrying with it associations of manliness and of sociability. This can extend from the hero who is simply seen as capable of taking a drink now and again, to the hero who uses his drinking (which may mean his capacity to drink substantial quantities without showing the effects of drinking) to assert his manliness. Further, because drinking is often shown as an activity which is undertaken in the company of others, the drinking hero can be seen to demonstrate his ability to communicate, to establish relationships and to achieve some kind of social integration. In this context, it is important to note the functional aspects of drinking, both in social terms (it works as a mechanism to initiate and manipulate relationships and to assert priorities within them) and in dramatic terms (it gives actors something to do with their hands). Whilst the latter function is clear enough, the former may require a word of explanation. Since, by its very nature, a film is required to schematise a version of an incident, or a cluster of incidents, which in sequence constitute a plot, into something which is played out in a relatively short space of time, it is often particularly appropriate to adopt, even to rely upon, certain social shorthands. One such shorthand or convention is the use of alcohol. It is easier for a character (as in real life) to open a relationship with a relative stranger if some mutually acceptable approach, such as the offer to buy a drink, can be used. Similarly, as a relationship develops, the use of drinking as a form of intimacy, or a form of granting approval, or as many other forms of assigning social values, can serve to focus the way in which one character is seen to relate to others. Thus, as a social and dramatic convention, the business of drinking, particularly in the company of others, is expedient for plot development. Given the wealth of judgemental associations which surround drinking styles, the way in which the hero is seen as drinking will provide a positive indication of his moral worth.

On the simplest level, the drinker remains in control, both of himself and of his drinking. The second image, by contrast, that of the *drunk,* the man who has lost control, tends to carry negative or, quite frequently, comic associations. It is only necessary to look at a film such as, for example, *The Thin Man* to see how drinking, even very frequent drinking, which does not lead to drunkenness is contrasted with drinking which does lead to drunkenness. The drunk becomes a pathetic figure who carries strong associations of inadequacy and who, in social terms, disrupts potential communications. He is, therefore, the other side of the coin to the drinker, even though the only manifest difference is that he shows the effects of his drinking.

It is, however, the third image, that of the *compulsive drinker,* which is most interesting and which has the greatest heroic significance. Although the drunk can certainly be used in thematic terms to focus attention on the essentially precarious nature of events, relying as it does upon a complex of mutually accepted codes of behaviour, the compulsive drinker sets himself up less as a chaotic or anarchic force and more as a fundamental antithesis of the values of the society from which he is generated. Although the behaviour of the drunk can lead to confusion and even to catastrophe, it lacks sufficient stature to achieve tragic outcome. The catastrophes produced by drunks are errors of circumstance, whilst the tragedies produced by compulsive drinkers are errors of action. It is the difference between a passive and an active relationship between the individual and society. The actions of a drunk may certainly impinge upon society and therefore society may wish to hold the drunk responsible, though usually his drunkenness is taken as a mitigating circumstance. His mistakes are the mistakes of a befuddled mind or a wayward body. Not so the compulsive drinker who, when drinking, reveals something of a true self that remains otherwise concealed. What happens when he makes a mistake is that the mistake represents the wrong choice he has made, whatever forces of destiny

The alcoholic hero: the hero alone (A Star is Born, USA 1954, Dir. George Cukor).

or ethanol he cares to cite in his favour. The choice is the choice of the individual, made with a clarity and a precision which characterise the best and the worst of acts.

Thomas Hardy, the novelist, described tragedy as 'the worthy encompassed by the inevitable'. In such terms, *The Lost Weekend* becomes something more than a dramatised documentary of one man's struggle against drink. It becomes a story about the violation of moral order and the process of expiation which is required for the re-assertion of that order. The alcoholic hero carries his destiny with him, constantly choosing yet forever denied freedom of choice. It is the ambivalence alluded to earlier, in which the alcoholic makes a choice to drink every time the opportunity presents itself and this, by the very behaviour itself, by its compulsive nature, demonstrates the illusion of choice. His alcoholism becomes a force greater than he can consciously control, yet he struggles against all that to maintain at least the style of being the man who knows what he wants. It is simply that his desire, even more than most, leads to tunnel vision. He expresses the final selfishness of the hero, in which the act of heroism becomes in the end more important than the reason it is undertaken. All that is required is that we recognise, in whatever terms, that the hero is worthy; that the hero carries the capacity to act with that laser-beam of single-mindedness which cuts across the neat rules of behaviour which normally determine the affairs of society. It is sometimes his compulsive drinking which sets him off sufficiently from his fellows to enable him to take this crucial last step.

Such a rigorous pursuit of self-fulfilment has about it the same compulsion as the drinking itself. Whether it is greed for power or greed for drink, it represents not so much a loss of will-power as a preposterous focusing of the will upon specific objects. Compare the compulsive drinker therefore with one of the coolest customers in recent literature. Pechorin from *A Hero of Our Times* says: 'My chief satisfaction is to subject everything around me to my will. Is not the first sight and the greatest triumph of power to be able to arouse feelings of love, devotion and fear towards ourselves? What is happiness but satisfied pride? The idea of evil cannot enter a man's head without his wanting to put it into practice.'

We are not expected to *like* a hero. There is nothing in the role which is required of them that recommends such a response. Indeed, the kind of detachment which Aristotle describes is remote from the cosy affection that an audience sometimes feels for the brave buffoons who, merely as a result of thoughtless courage, crave heroic status. The compulsive drinker, therefore, starts with an advantage, since we learn early on that he is not trustworthy. Who would trust Othello, after all, or even Hamlet? Look where that led Rosencranz and Guildenstern. Not that Othello or Hamlet are shown as compulsive drinkers. But they do demonstrate tragic flaws of the same order and are equally swept along by a destiny which, although it is of their own making, is not within their control.

It is, of course, always some final cataclysmic act of will which saves them all. So Dean Martin and not John Wayne is the real hero of *Rio Bravo*. Thinking of the three images described earlier in this chapter, John Wayne is the drinker; and a very fine figure he is, knocking it back appropriately and adopting generally a high moral stance towards drunkenness. He does well during the film, certainly, but who would ever have doubted it? Dean Martin, on the other hand, when he pours the whisky back into the bottle (a conventional enough gesture) fights against forces which are much more difficult to surmount than a rabble of cheap gunslingers. For it is salvation, after all, which motivates the hero and which drives him on through his selfishness. 'To will it when the spirit cries in torment—that is to find salvation,' wrote Sophocles and nowhere is that more ably demonstrated than in the comparison between John Wayne and Dean Martin. At no point in the film does John Wayne face a moral dilemma, because he is always perfectly clear in his mind what his duty is. No doubts cloud the issue for him and personal issues, like the tantalising relationship with Angie Dickinson, take second place. He has started something which he is going to finish and therefore, of course, he plays the part of leader superbly, doing the right thing and making the right judgements on cue. Dean Martin, on the other hand, is lost, caught between his drinking and his good intentions. The old notion of the hero's tragic flaw is easy to apply here. All the good intentions in the world are irrelevant to his compulsion until he makes the proud, vain, foolish, heroic choice to step outside the role he has been playing and actually take a real active hand in the action. His dilemma is not one of survival in terms of life expectancy but of survival in terms of ontological force.

It is a heroic quality which is, for example, never really achieved by Stacy Keach in his portrayal of the alcoholic private eye Naboth in *The Squeeze*.

The alcoholic hero: the hero alone (Rio Bravo, USA 1959, Dir. Howard Hawks).

Partly, that is because *The Squeeze,* for all its circumstantiality, is an episodic and casual drama which lacks the linear, almost allegorical simplicity of *Rio Bravo.* Partly, of course, this can be explained by the difference in genre between the films, but it has to do also with their heroic possibilities, or lack of them. It is not that heroes should not be seen running down the street naked except for a pair of shoes held over their private parts; it is rather that such a stripping of conventional dignity requires that there should be underneath a much more fundamental and intransigent kind of dignity. Instead, in the case of Naboth, there is a kind of bluff sentimentality which is closer to the screen image of the drunk than to the image of the compulsive drinker.

What emerges, therefore, from this brief discussion of the alcoholic hero is that the lowest common denominator of their heroism is that they should transcend their alcoholism. Yet, perversely, it is their compulsive drinking which opens the door for them to heroic action. Equally, it is hardly enough to stop

The alcoholic hero: the hero alienated from his world (A Star is Born, USA 1954, Dir. George Cukor).

drinking. That is, at best, commendable only and, at worst, banal. The cessation (since the movies still run a decade or two behind the scientific evidence and have therefore not yet come to terms with the concept of controlled drinking by recovered alcoholics) is required to relate to specific forms of action which permit the protagonist to demonstrate what Hardy would have called his *worth*. Nor is this, of course, the only issue on which the movies lag rather behind the scientific evidence. It cannot be explained simply on the grounds that film makers are not regular readers of the *Quarterly Journal of Studies on Alcohol*. It is rather that the biting point for a film is the point where its view and that of its audience meet. The world and the film world thus create each other. Experimental evidence that seeks to alter the perceived interpretation shared by both these worlds is hardly likely to be welcomed. Audiences, through distributors, see the films which they deserve.

Nobody should be so naive as to suppose that there is heroic potential in every derelict who shambles along past the National Film Theatre with a meths bottle swinging from his hand. At the same time, it is difficult to deny the curious mythic force of people like Dylan Thomas or John Berryman, choosing (the phrase is not accidental) to drink themselves to death. It is not, after all, just what is done that makes a man a hero. The same event set in different circumstances can be truly tragic or mindlessly inept. It is the quality of the experience on offer to the audience, who can participate and observe simultaneously, which determines its significance. When Dean Martin conquers his withdrawal symptoms so that he can pour the whisky back without spilling it, he is demonstrating that he can control a great deal more than his drinking. At that moment, and it is the moment which redeems the hero, he controls the world.

Women, Alcohol and the Screen

by Judith Harwin and Shirley Otto

In one field I think women would do well to avoid equality with men. I have in mind alcoholism. There is something formidable and tragic about any alcoholic but the female variety is really terrible. Nothing more fatally draws attention to this than a film having as its heroine a lush—as the Americans describe a lady afflicted with this malady—unless it is animated by a spirit of compassionate enquiry, intelligent analysis or art. (From a contemporary *Daily Mail* film review of *Too Much Too Soon* by Fred Majdalany.)

Few films have been made about women alcoholics, many fewer than have been made about male alcoholics. In fact 15 such films are listed in Halliwell's *Filmgoers' Companion,* eight of which were made during the late forties to early sixties and six during the late sixties. Why there should be this lack of interest in women alcoholics (and open hostility to the subject amongst some critics) is open to speculation as no systematic studies have as yet been made. However, despite this, it is still worthwhile to examine some of the possible reasons.

Predictably, one of the most influential phenomena in shaping the representation of women alcoholics on film has been the stigma associated with alcoholism in women. This stigma has as a consequence ensured that many such women remained hidden from public view and therefore, in effect, limited the possibility of any broader portrayal than that derived from a minority of highly atypical women who drank in public, such as actresses and prostitutes. It is only comparatively recently in the late sixties and early seventies that the significant increase in the incidence of alcoholism amongst women has forcibly brought to the attention of the public the fact that the majority of women with alcoholism problems live at home and lead apparently normal lives.

It is our aim in this chapter to explore the assumptions and ideologies that inform the filmic representations of alcoholic women. Our analysis is based on seven films and is made from the point of view of people primarily concerned with alcohol problems.

Part one discusses the portrayal of women alcoholics in this selection of films. This is followed by an account of the degree of congruence of the cinematic representation of women alcoholics with the various prevailing contemporary notions about alcoholism in women.

Part two is concerned with the relationship of these films to other contemporary films representing women as primary and secondary characters and continues by considering the motivation for their production. Finally, we consider whether films about women alcoholics are more usefully located within the genre of the 'women's film', that is, films aimed at women, featuring

37

women as central protagonists, which have been regarded as affirming women in their traditional roles.

Part one

The Representations
The most striking feature underlying the representations in the films studied was the marked uniformity of characterisation. Despite inhabiting quite different social worlds, from the glamour of Hollywood to the underworld of petty crime and prostitution, whether major or secondary characters, all are desperately unhappy and lonely women who lack all self-confidence. Three of them, Lillian Roth in *I'll Cry Tomorrow*, Diana Barrymore in *Too Much, Too Soon* and Kirstie Clay in *Days of Wine and Roses* have started out life with many advantages. United by their good looks, money or fame, they each gradually become as seedy, degraded and pathetic as the two shadowy and faded lushes in *Key Largo* and *Farewell My Lovely*. As the mask of youth and good fortune deserts them, Diana, Lillian, and Kirstie are gradually stripped and exposed as helpless, passive and vulnerable individuals, who desperately seek affirmation from others, using their sexuality in order to gain some kind of self-validation.

These women are their own worst enemies: but they also have the power to destroy others. Diana Barrymore is the most eloquent illustration of this. In her search for security, she creates a prison first for her father and then for her husband. When she loses both she immediately gives herself up to a succession of casual affairs, each time trying to find her own identity, or more accurately, to escape from an identity she finds abhorrent. The tragedy for these women is that they have insight into their own psychopathology, but are unable to overcome this without first sinking to their nadir.

Lonely, destructive, dependent and restless—the characterisation is starkly negative and can evoke in the spectator at best sympathy and pity, and at worst impatience and contempt.

Male and Female Alcoholic Compared
Such representations, which cluster so consistently for a twenty-five year period around the same negative attributes, inevitably force comparison with the depiction of the male alcoholic.

Although the figure of the alcoholic woman is less popular in the cinema than that of the alcoholic man, nevertheless there are certain broad similarities in their portrayal. Previous chapters have drawn attention to the dramatic potential inherent in the subject of alcoholism. Not just is there the dramatic scope for unexpected reversals of fortune to be found in the possibility of relapse, there is also a deeper symbolism contained in the moral struggle which the attempt for the mastery of alcoholism represents—it symbolizes the struggle of the human will. When this theme is made manifest by an especially gifted individual as hero, the drama begins to resemble the heroism of classical tragedy. But the similarities in subject matter hide significant ideological differences.

For the female alcoholics, who appear to have brilliant careers as singers and actresses with all the trappings of glamour and public acclaim, are misfits within their roles. Diana Barrymore, with her one ambition to become as great a star as her father, is patently ungifted; Lillian Roth *is* gifted and successful but desperately craves not public acclaim but personal fulfilment and love from her boyfriend.

These women are not autonomous either in their choice of career or continuation within it. Rather they are cast into their parts to fulfil the ambitions of others. The opening line of *I'll Cry Tomorrow* immediately underlines the theme of the film: 'My life was never my own—it was charted before I was born.' Precisely because they had not chosen their own careers, any sense of value within their role comes not from within, nor from public acclaim, but from parental approval. Lillian Roth is jealously watched by her mother in all her performances, and Lillian's first question is always to seek her mother's opinion. Thus although outwardly they appear women of talent and independence, inwardly they remain insecure children motivated by desire to gain parental approval. The only way they discover to resolve this dilemma is through alcohol.

The low status of the female alcoholic emerges even more sharply in those films where male and female alcoholics co-exist. Both *Too Much, Too Soon* and *Days of Wine and Roses* provide an ideal opportunity to compare the treatment of and attitude towards male and female alcoholics. The differences are dramatic. Although alcoholism finally kills John Barrymore he nonetheless continues to charm and command attention. Where his entrances are most feared, he steals the show. At the party in honour of the launching of Diana's first film, her father arrives uninvited, refuses the soft drink carefully proferred to him by the discomforted producer, pours himself champagne and proceeds to captivate the entire company with his suavity and talent as raconteur. But he has the last laugh. For he never drinks the champagne. His control is total. Diana is totally eclipsed and is happy to be so, basking in reflected glory.

Earlier chapters have noted that the spectacle of male drunkenness is often humorous or physically commanding. When women are drunk it is nearly always degrading. Only in one very recent film, *Opening Night* (1978, Dir. John Cassavetes) is female drunkenness esteemed and allowed to generate creativity in the protagonist and to entertain the audience. The film's climax comes when the heroine, played by Gena Rowlands, arrives late and drunk at the theatre on the opening night of a new play in which she is the main star. But behind the drunken, seemingly incapable exterior, her control is complete. Indeed, her drunken demeanour becomes the vehicle to turn the fate of the play's menopausal heroine from tragedy to comedy, thereby refuting the protrayal of loss and despair in the original conception of the play. It is a personal triumph for Gena Rowlands, who has been until this moment unable to act the part because of her own identification with the empty future of the play's heroine, a future which she also faces.

Significantly, this is the only sequence where a woman alcoholic is congratulated on her capacity to handle a vast quantity of liquor. As a stage hand turns to her he remarks, 'I've seen a lot of drunks in my time, but I haven't seen one as drunk as you and able to handle it so well.'

But the most telling comparison of all lies in *Days of Wine and Roses,* where husband and wife both become submerged by their alcoholism. Each locks the other into a destructive and desperate relationship. Joe Clay (whose own drinking is problematic from the outset) first introduces Kirstie to alcohol. She by contrast moves from the position of being a teetotaller into someone unable to give up. The different methods of handling their own drinking problem highlight the way in which sexual identity repeatedly shapes the characters' personalities, and thus the pattern of their lives. For Kirstie, having slipped passively into a drinking career, with equal passivity cannot pull herself out, apart from a single attempt to give up following the birth of her child. Thereafter it is Joe who makes the decision to give up and who, despite set-backs, finally succeeds. Indeed, by the end of the film Joe has found himself. At the beginning he is full of self-disgust and journeys along a path of increasing self-degradation, losing his job, undermining his marriage and hating himself for his behaviour. By the end, he holds a stable job and is acting as father and mother to the child and appears to have found some inner contentment. By contrast Kirstie never fully emerges from the world of alcoholism and, unable to see where she might belong, remains an outsider who is therefore unable to re-enter the world of family and home life. Thus we are asked to see Kirstie as the more disturbed of the two partners, whose future at the end of the film remains highly equivocal. It might be argued that male alcoholics are shown equally damaged. John Barrymore after all dies from alcohol. Yet his self-destruction co-exists with creativity and charisma. There is no counterbalancing gift to redeem the female alcoholic and, repeatedly, female alcoholism is shown to embody a cluster of entirely negative attributes. Perhaps the reason for this is that the fatal flaw of the woman alcoholic is that she is a woman, and can therefore never transcend herself.

Alcoholism Explained

It has already been shown how gender shapes the depiction of the female alcoholic. Gender also sheds some light in explaining why the protagonists become alcoholic. In the three films with a female alcoholic as heroine considerable attention is devoted to their early upbringing, with scenes from childhood and adolescence sketched in. By contrast early autobiographical detail is markedly absent in the portrayal of male alcoholic heroes, whose alcoholism is explained in terms of the interaction between their personalities and current social worlds, rather than their childhood. For example in *Rio Bravo* we learn that Dude began drinking after a broken love affair but there is no mention of his early childhood experiences. Only in *Come Fill the Cup* is there a brief cameo in which a dominating over-protective mother is offered as the cause for her talented, pianist son's alcohol abuse. But broadly speaking, the male alcoholic emerges as autonomous, freed from the ties of his childhood.

The patterning and stereotyping of the female alcoholic emerge even more sharply when one examines the characteristics of the homes in which Kirstie,

The alcoholic woman and her father (Days of Wine and Roses, USA 1962, Dir. Blake Edwards).

Diana and Lillian grew up. The latter two are strikingly similar. The overriding preoccupation with parents is a major theme—clearly intended to explain the pathology of Diana and Lillian. Both are the children of divorced parents, with dominant, ambitious mothers and soft or absent fathers. The relationships that Diana and Lillian form with their parents are consistently shown to be pathological. Diana is locked in an oedipal relationship with both parents, desperately competing with her mother to secure the exclusive attention of her father. In his final months of life she looks after him with the passionate jealousy of a lover rather than a daughter. It is a psychopathology so overt as to even be noticed by other characters in the film; hence at the start of the film Diana's boyfriend asks her, 'Don't you think it's about time you stopped chasing your father and began living your own life?'

But this is just what she cannot do. After her father's death she continues her unconscious and compulsive pattern of caging those who become close to her. She begs her husband not to leave her for a business trip because she 'needs someone all the time'. She suffocates her boyfriend in a desperate attempt to escape from her inner loneliness and isolation. Where this fails, alcohol provides comfort and escape.

Yet why should Kirstie Clay, whose childhood was stable with an extremely happy parental relationship, become alcoholic? Initially it is hard to see in her the gross personality disturbance that characterise Lillian and Diana. Yet there are common traits. For the greed and insatiability which dominate their relation-

41

ship is shown in a different form with Kirstie. A seemingly unimportant shot of her at the beginning of the film shows her at work, eating a bar of chocolate. Only near the end of the film does the purpose of the scene become clear, when an AA member comments that her compulsive chocolate-eating and greedy orality were a pointer to her subsequent development of a drinking problem. So this film too, although made some years later than *Too Much Too Soon,* still attributes much explanatory force to Freudian psychology as a significant factor in explaining Kirstie's alcoholism.

Female Alcoholism—A Changing Perspective?

It would be wrong to overemphasise the similarities in explanatory models used by *Too Much, Too Soon; I'll Cry Tomorrow,* and *Days of Wine and Roses.* The last film offers a far more complex set of possible causes for the predicament of its protagonists, and in this way shows how the representations do alter over time. These can be understood more fully by looking at the films' endings. The films divide again into those made in the 1950s (*I'll Cry Tomorrow* and *Too Much, Too Soon*) and the later *Days of Wine and Roses.* It will be clear from the preceding analysis that if the alcoholism of Lillian and Diana is explained in terms of their immaturity, their need for immediate gratification, their vanity and self-doubt, so the road to recovery must lie in the mastery of these defects. Diana's 'cure' does not come until the end of the film when she is finally able to stand alone and gently turn down a marriage proposal from her former beau, Link, because she no longer 'needs someone all the time'. With her discovery that Link has grown bald, her own vanity and narcissism fall away as she laughingly realises that 'I guess I'm not the only one life's played dirty tricks on'.

Throughout these two films both heroines are 'takers', whether using their sexuality to seduce, or appealing to others through their own desperate vulnerability and child-like needs. It is only when they can learn to 'give' that they attain self-mastery. Lillian Roth's final comments in the film underline the point: 'You get by giving and you only get by giving.'

The loss of narcissism represents more than the strengthening of personality; rather it symbolises the triumph of morality. It reminds us of the link between moral discourse and alcoholism and that until comparatively recently alcoholism belonged to the realm of morals rather than science. It also illustrates the way in which the films operate within a dual and seemingly contradictory framework, in that we are asked both to exculpate the heroines for their alcoholism because of the unhappiness of their early years, and yet to judge their stature in terms of their capacity to control their own destinies by self-mastery. What is perhaps most noticeable is the fact that whilst the model of alcoholism evolves, the depiction of the female alcoholic remains essentially static.

Yet despite a dual framework, the films show a striking internal logic which perhaps is best illustrated in the type of treatment which is shown to be most helpful. Not surprisingly AA emerges as the most potent treatment force. For if alcoholism is shown to centre on inner loneliness, self-doubt and self-hate, then successful treatment must ultimately lie not in the provision of drugs, nor in the alteration of the social order, but rather in the capacity to offer warm

The alcoholic woman and her father (Too Much, Too Soon, USA 1958, Dir. Art Napoleon).

and caring relationships to others. AA with its readiness to give the individual as much time and attention as she seeks is probably the only 'treatment' organisation to emphasise so heavily the primacy of human relationships, as well as to stress that selfishness, egocentricity and wild striving all carry within them the seeds of alcoholism. Institutional care by contrast, emerges as inhumane and uncaring, ready to turn its inmates onto the street with neither money nor home.

But the ideology operates in a far more complex way in *Days of Wine and Roses*. Are we to see Kirstie's inability to 'come home' at the end as failure or triumph? When Kirstie walks away from husband and child saying 'you'd better give up on me' are we to see this as an indication of her immaturity in which she cannot cope with the role of wife and mother? Has Kirstie held up the mirror to the dreariness of everyday life symbolised by her husband's recovery in her despairing comment—'the world looks so dirty to me when I'm not drinking'? The antithesis within these two possible interpretations represents the duality of the film. Throughout it is built on a series of contrasts: the rural simplicity of Kirstie's childhood symbolised by her father's horticulture; the massive complexity of city life symbolised by Joe Clay's work in advertising. The bright lights of the city; the greyness of everyday life. And finally the world of alcohol and the world of sobriety. Kirstie herself embodies this duality; is she a 'dead soul' or is the world around her dead?

Although this film in many ways is a marked departure from the other two, all nonetheless share a primary interest in the personality structure and inner world of the heroines. Why should this be?

Theoretical Perspectives

An examination of the academic literature of the period provides some useful guidelines. Whilst there is a considerable range of aetiological models used, including social learning, biochemical and sociocultural explanations, there is some evidence that psychodynamic theories predominated in the forties and fifties and even into the sixties in the USA. These laid heavy emphasis on disturbances in early childhood relationships. In turn these were frequently linked to the development of a specific personality type—namely the oral personality, who because of lack of love in childhood compulsively craves oral satisfaction in adult life, and is unable to form mature relationships.

Menninger[1] takes the theme of childhood deprivation one stage further in its relationship to alcoholism:

Alcoholics unconsciously have a powerful urge to destroy themselves. Addiction is the one means of expressing this unconscious urge, which is the result of the child's feeling betrayed by the parents. The frustration arising from the betrayal results in an intense rage which in turn causes interpersonal conflict. He wishes to destroy his parents, yet he fears losing them. Later in life alcohol becomes a means of achieving both gratification and revenge against the parents. The feeling of hostility towards parents creates a desire for punishment to alleviate guilt.

The particular quotation could have been the author's notes to actresses for both Lillian and Diana, with rather fainter echoes for Kirstie Clay.

The academic literature of the period tended to disagree on the importance of gender in aetiology and outcome. One writer, Block,[2] rejects male/female differences, stating that 'the key factor is whether people are well-adjusted or not and can cope with problems in living'. Karpman,[3] writing fourteen years earlier in 1948, takes the opposite point of view. He states: 'What alcoholic women seem to lack in quantity, they certainly seem to make up in quality. By clinical observation they are much more abnormal than alcoholic men. . . .'

However, perhaps the most striking fact to emerge from a review of the literature is not the disagreements about the properties of male and female alcoholism, but the overwhelming lack of discussion on the topic. It is therefore somewhat paradoxical that the aetiological factors explored so fully in the films' accounts of female alcoholism refer in the *academic* literature principally to men. Some of these, principally the psychodynamic explanations, show a

The alcoholic woman—self-loathing and degradation (I'll Cry Tomorrow, USA 1955, Dir. Daniel Mann).

remarkable closeness to the accounts offered 'in the films, had they been describing the origins of female alcoholism.

Yet these same explanations are rarely explored in the cinema portrayal of the male alcoholic. Is this yet another example of stereotyping whereby the representation of women in *general* is inextricably bound up with the small personal world of family relationships—a world which is held to be inappropriate for males to inhabit?

Thus we are faced with some very real contradictions. On the one hand we have seen that the cinematic representation of the female alcoholic is consistently narrow, stereotyped and static, embodying essentially the negative attributes of vulnerability, dependency and, at times, destructiveness. Such a portrayal is consistent with the imagery which dominates the academic literature. But that literature was also intended to describe the male alcoholic, who as we have seen, is nonetheless permitted in the cinematic representations a far wider range of attributes and positive qualities. Why then should the woman alcoholic be presented in such a totally negative way? It is at this point that a study of the academic literature on alcoholism ceases to explain fully the depiction of the woman alcoholic in the cinema.

Part two

The fact that there is little literature available on the representation of women

The alcoholic woman–self-loathing and degradation (I'll Cry Tomorrow, USA 1955, Dir. Daniel Mann).

in films at all other than 'elegies to tragic movie queens or homages to sex goddesses' limits the degree to which it is possible to examine the role of an even more unseen group, women alcoholics. However, within these confines we offer below an analysis of the changing representation of women alcoholics as compared with women *per se* in the cinema, and reflect on the motivation for making films about such an unpopular topic at all.

Women, Women Alcoholics and the Cinema
(i) The Forties
The impression gained of women in films in the forties is of the declining years of a golden age in which, to use Molly Haskell's term, women were 'revered'. It was the era of Bette Davis, Joan Crawford and Katharine Hepburn, amongst others. It was a time when 'women are seen as partners to men, as their equals in initiative and courage'.[4] This era in film history was terminated by certain brutal economic realities in which women faced massive redundancy as men returned from war to reclaim their jobs. Along with this economic change, the general ideological necessity to reconstruct women more traditionally was reflected particularly in the representation in film, such that the once dominant woman, the strong protagonist, became 'the background buffoon, love object, or thorn in her man's side. Gone were attempts at recreating lives of intriguing women'.[5]

46

Although these strong pro-women forces were in decline, it is perhaps not surprising that one of the rare films in which a woman alcoholic is seen as heroic was in a film made at this time. In *Key Largo* the bar room background of the alcoholic played by Claire Trevor who has clearly seen better days is contrasted with the apparent wholesomeness of Lauren Bacall, shown living with her father-in-law after the death of her husband in the war.

After what Molly Haskell[4] describes as 'one of the most degrading scenes in the cinema . . . when Edward G. Robinson makes Claire Trevor, his boozy mistress and an ex-singer, suffer through a torch song to get a drink' this woman alcoholic gambles her life to steal a gun from her ex-boyfriend and give it to Humphrey Bogart, thereby dashing the hopes of the gangsters. It is significant that this portrayal of a woman alcoholic was acceptable to film critics otherwise hostile to such representations. For example, the reviewer in the *Daily Mail* wrote: 'The one character who does stand out is the aging moll, brilliantly played by Claire Trevor, who gives a beautifully judged impression of a faded showgirl, broken by her life with the gangster, and a slave to the bottle.'

(ii) The Fifties

The first era of prosperity and peace since the twenties opened with women pressured 'out of the employment market and into conjugal bliss'.[5] The priorities for women were clearly for home and hearth. So called 'women's films' became even further divorced from controversial themes and tended to concentrate on 'catching and keeping a man'.

Marjorie Rosen draws attention to the fact that 'throughout the fifties the female artist/actress consistently chose, or was forced to reconsider, marriage over theatrical ambitions. Bette . . . prances around like a sexy ingenue . . . before she learns she has neglected "being a woman first"',[5] (in the film *The Star*, 1952). Indeed, women maintaining vital lifestyles, that is in many cases careers, were in consequence punished by being assigned characteristics often both pathetic and neurotic, bitchy and insatiable; rolled into one these become the terms of the representation of alcoholism in women.

The glamorous 'real' lives of the stars are used both to sell the films and also to point out the moral that a career is not a means by which women can find their fulfilment (e.g. *I'll Cry Tomorrow; Too Much, Too Soon*). The portrayals were less full than of the women in the forties and showed a sex all too easily unbalanced by emotional forces especially outside the home or homely environment.

(iii) The Sixties

It is significant that in the sixties when so many taboos broke down there were still very few films made about alcoholism in women. This is despite the resurgence of controversial themes in films, largely through the influence of the European cinema and reflected in films such as *Room at the Top* and *Look Back in Anger* which brought a new frankness even to commercial cinema. The concept of an adult film, as opposed to a family film, allowed the kind of exploration of marital difficulties well portrayed in the one key alcoholism film of this decade, *Days of Wine and Roses*. This film differs from the others portraying women alcoholics in that alcoholism problems occur within the framework of a marriage, an alcoholic marriage, where the husband, unlike those in the fifties films, is devoted. However, the visual presentation of Kirstie's decline is presented in ways similar to Diana Barrymore's and Lillian Roth's. Each of these films, and indeed *Farewell My Lovely* (1975), another portrayal of an alcoholic woman filmed in the seventies, seem informed by some archetype in which a drunken woman is sluttishly dressed, or undressed to be more correct, living in seedy unkempt circumstances, usually having gone to fat and facially older than her years. The overtones usually indicate sexual degradation of a kind that comes about when a woman has lost her self-respect and knows that she has lost everyone else's. In other words, the portrayal of the drunken woman is a stereotype which has not changed at least over the last 20 years despite change both in ideas about alcoholism and in the nature of the portrayal of women. Whatever in reality might be the case, drunkenness is closely associated in the minds of the media with a woman's abuse of her sexuality. The woman has lost control of herself, through drinking, and has therefore lost some essential femininity.

This brief analysis of women and women alcoholics in films from the forties to the present day suggests that the films under scrutiny were largely consonant with their time in terms of the prevailing values and assumptions about women's roles. However, at the same time, it is also clear that the portrayal of the women when drunk (at least at the later stages of their problem), reflect a persistent and deeply felt association between drunkenness and sexuality in women.

To have portrayed the women as alcoholics was unusual, particularly in the fifties when the audience might well be hostile to the notion of alcoholism in women. This raises the question as to why these films were made by commercial concerns who must have anticipated there would be sufficient people who would pay for the pleasure of watching them. It is quite possible that at least *I'll Cry Tomorrow* and *Too Much, Too Soon* might be understood within a category called a 'woman's film'.

A 'woman's film' is defined by Molly Haskell thus: 'In the woman's film, the woman—a woman—is the centre of the universe.'[4] The woman's film is the equivalent to the male adventure film—particularly the western—for each sex is entertained by those characteristics most typically associated with their stereotypes. To quote Molly Haskell again:

> Basically, the woman's film is no more maudlin or self-pitying than the male adventure film, (the male weepie), particularly in the male films' recent mood of bronco busting buddies and blurry-eyed nostalgia. The well of self-pity in both types of films, though only hinted at, is bottomless, and in their sublimation or evasion of adult reality, they reveal, almost by accident, their attitudes towards marriage—disillusion, frustration and contempt—beneath the sunnyside-up philosophy concealed in the happy ending.

It is clear from this that Haskell considers that the woman's film has political as well as personal implications for, to her mind, the women on the screen act for the women watching the film as 'audience surrogates, the heroines are defined negatively and collectively by their mutual limitations rather than their talent or aspirations'. The motivation then behind these films is 'not to encourage women to rebel or question their role, but to reconcile them to it, and thus preserve the *status quo*'. It would be true to say that most of the films we have discussed could be understood to be within the category of 'a women's film' as they show women's essential emotionality, vulnerability and need for strong, close personal relationships, particularly with men. They are often victims of themselves and of life with little self-determination, self-confidence, or autonomy.

Authenticity and the Modern Perspective

The key to our contemporary understanding of alcoholism in women is the low self-esteem and poor sense of identity which are manifest in the consistent evidence that many women are not only shown to have alcoholism problems but also to be very depressed. They are very likely to have had parents who had alcoholism problems, mothers with depression and have brothers or sisters who are also alcoholics. They, too, are likely to marry men who are either alcoholic or become so. Hence, the points that emerged out of the analysis in the first section, which highlighted the women's emotional vulnerability, their powerful need for affirmation and excessive dependency on men, are not inconsistent with our modern view. However, what is missing from these films is any sociological explanation as to why women should be so emotionally vulnerable and inadequate. Little is made of the powerful social mores and expectations that shaped the women's view of themselves as consumers of alcohol and ultimately as alcoholics, or of the ways in which the various mores are transmitted by lay and professional people to the woman who is at one point a drunkard and at another, an alcoholic.

In Conclusion

Have the films that portrayed women alcoholics been 'animated by a spirit of compassionate enquiry, intelligent analysis or art'? The answer must be, on the whole, that they have not. For not only are there few representations of women alcoholics in film but what portrayals there are lack variety and fail to command respect from the viewer. In this sense, men and women alcoholics are not treated equally; both are shown to have considerable problems but the men are allowed mitigation.

The films are interesting in that they reflect many of the prevailing assumptions about women and about women alcoholics. The problem is not what is shown but what is not, for it is possible to see representations of male alcoholics who are at the same time strong and creative or who have at least been so. This is not the case for a woman alcoholic, which seems to stem more from the fact of their gender than their condition. It is the lack of representation of these strengths that potentially both undermines a balanced view of women's problems and reinforces the negative and stereotyped view of women and of a woman's condition.

Notes

[1] K. A. Menninger, *Man Against Himself*, Harcourt, Brace and World, New York, 1938.
[2] M. Block, *Alcoholism: Its Facets and Phases*, John Day & Co. Inc., New York, 1962.
[3] B. Karpman, *The Alcoholic Woman*, Linacre Press, 1948.
[4] Molly Haskell, *From Reverence to Rape: The Treatment of Women in the Movies*, Penguin, USA, 1974.
[5] Marjorie Rosen, *Popcorn Venus: Women, Movies and the American Dream*, Avon, New York, 1973.

Images of Treatment

by Bruce Ritson

If I were worried that I was becoming an alcoholic and decided to seek help on the basis of the films about alcoholism which I had seen, I would know that I must avoid hospital at all costs. For someone who has been involved in the hospital treatment of alcoholism for some time, I am naturally concerned that the public image as represented in the cinema is so bizarre. The treatment of alcohol related problems is in fact a major concern, involving many different agencies and considerable sums of money. For instance, the Bay area in California invests approximately three million dollars a year in alcoholism treatment and yet many of the films focus on the work of a voluntary organisation which can be organised with no funds at all. The aim here then is to look at the discrepancy between the professional, social and institutional responses to alcohol related problems and the way in which the treatment agencies are portrayed in film.

Throughout our viewing, it is important to be conscious of the historical and geographic placing of each film. Fashions both in the concept of and the social response to alcoholism have changed considerably in recent decades. The films themselves represent and reflect these changing fashions.

Any discussion of treatment agencies must be conscious of geography and history. There is ample evidence that the disabilities associated with heavy drinking differ from place to place. Nations differ in their patterns of drinking and the way in which they perceive alcohol related problems. The majority of films which the conference considered represent the North American scene and are rooted in WASP culture.

The treatment agencies seen as appropriate for alcoholics have changed considerably over time. This is reflected in the transition from the prison-like drunk ward of *Lost Weekend* to the more hospital-like surroundings of recent films, e.g. *The Squeeze*.

Despite widespread acceptance of the disease concept of alcoholism, medical treatment does not seem to offer much beyond control and sedation. My own memory of treatment episodes in alcoholism films becomes a blur of needles, burly attendants, locked doors and terrifying screams. Delirium tremens is thought to occur in approximately 5% of alcoholics—the films show delirium and particularly hallucinations as a part of most alcoholics' experiences. The reason for this distortion presumably is the dramatic appeal of the symptoms and their horrifying quality. They are usually shown in a highly exaggerated form unlike anything I have personally witnessed. What may seem laughable to those who have experienced the real situation—for instance the straight jacket scene in *Days of Wine and Roses* — may prove upsetting to those who may be contemplating treatment for themselves, or have relatives whom they are trying to persuade to seek help. There is no reason why film makers should be unduly conscious of the sensitivities of such minorities but it is worth speculating about the effects of such scenes. They may also reassure problem drinkers that they are certainly not 'like that' and that it is therefore safe to carry on drinking. The DT's scenes are powerful images and reflect and perpetuate an unfortunate stereotype about alcoholism. Another reason for choosing them may be to convey as tersely as possible that this person's drinking is different. Alcohol withdrawal symptoms, briefly and rather more accurately, are shown in a recent film *The Squeeze* to make a point quickly about the hero's drinking problem that separates him off from other drinkers and makes the viewer aware that this is an additional handicap that he has to overcome.

Apart from drying out, films tell us little about treatment or treatment agencies. In *The Squeeze* we are shown a parody of the behavioural psychiatrist at work. In the treatment scene the patient is seated some twenty feet from the therapists. He wears head phones wired up to an apparatus that emits what seems to be a painful shrieking sound when he tries to drink. He is forced to go on drinking despite the attendant discomfort and there is no hint of an inter-personal relationship; the diabolic machine is all that is offered. The treatment shown has no foundation in fact; it is, rather, a dramatic expression of the psychiatrist's alienation from the person he is trying to help. Indeed, aversion therapy is shown as a battle of wills which is, of course, in keeping with the anti-psychiatry fashion of the time. The only advantage the hero gets from the hospital is a sexual relationship with a nurse who steps outside her professional role.

Those films which have focused on alcoholism as a central issue describe the hero or heroine as having some flaw in their personality. This usually is supposed to arise from a significant life trauma, for instance, the polio victim's 'quarrel with fate' in *I'll Cry Tomorrow*. In addition to overcoming the addiction the hero has to heal these psychic scars so that the films commonly focus first on decline, with hospital treatment and skid row seen as the low point and with recovery effected by means of a relationship. In many films of this kind this miracle is achieved by Alcoholics Anonymous, usually with the conspicuous involvement of a single member. Despite the existence of several other agencies concerned with alcoholics, such as councils on alcoholism, psychiatric clinics and some social work counselling services, it is Alcoholics Anonymous which has captured the film maker's imagination.

Alcoholics Anonymous was founded in 1935 in the USA by two alcoholics who felt that alcoholics needed to support each other in the face of their addic-tion, public apathy and professional ignorance. The movement has been extremely successful in purveying a particular concept of alcoholism—for instance that it is a disease and that for the established alcoholic 'one drink is one too many and a thousand not enough'. It remains the best known agency for alcoholics—recent surveys in Britain have demonstrated that amongst doctors and the general public AA is the only treatment facility that is widely known. In portraying AA as the only known effective agency the film maker is reflecting public opinion. Recognition that many other effective agencies and treatment methods exist has not reached the cinema. It is interesting that a wide range of other therapeutic approaches have been neglected or portrayed as of no value.

Treatment: the keeper (A Star is Born, USA 1954, Dir. George Cukor).

If the viewer is influenced by these films in deciding about the way in which he should respond either to his own drinking problem or that of a friend, he would feel that Alcoholics Anonymous and a life of total abstinence was the only answer. This image may unfortunately make it easy for someone to ignore the fact that they are seriously harming themselves with drink, because of the popular image of the alcoholic as someone who cannot control his drinking and is always drinking. As one patient said recently, 'I can't be an alcoholic, doctor, because I never drink on Sundays.'

The importance of a healing relationship may provide an additional clue to the film makers' predilection for AA. We can see that the AA meetings with their enthusiasm and stress on group identification processes and the importance attached to saying publicly 'I am an alcoholic' have a compelling dramatic quality. The meeting is often portrayed as the turning point in the process of coming to admit that alcoholism is the problem. While the AA meeting is the place where the defeat of the villain (the demon drink) is celebrated, it is in the working through of a relationship that this celebration is made possible. Films, and for that matter books, on which many are based, understandably feel happiest in portraying change occurring as a result of a new relationship in which both members are free of constraints, free to explore each other. This effectively excludes focusing on a professional-client relationship and makes most other treatment modalities unsatisfactory dramatic material.

The professional therapist is confined in films to a role which does not

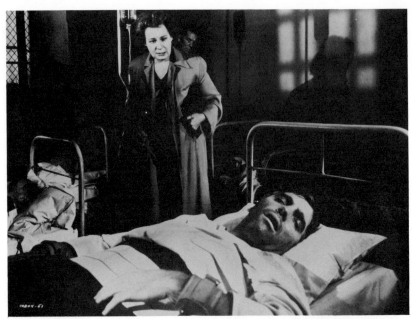

Treatment: drying out (Come Back Little Sheba, USA 1952, Dir. Daniel Mann).

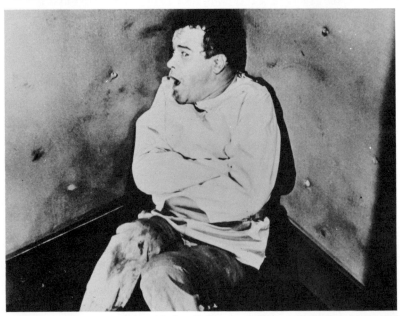

Treatment: DT's and the padded cell (Days of Wine and Roses, USA 1962, Dir. Blake Edwards).

Treatment: the Alcoholics Anonymous confessional (I'll Cry Tomorrow, USA 1955, Dir. Daniel Mann).

require serious exploration of his own nature, he is a caricature, physically restraining, injecting, maintaining distance, and departing from his professional role by being sadistic or manipulative. The representation of the client-therapist relationship in a successful form is not attempted in these films.

Alcoholics Anonymous again provides an answer to this dilemma—two individuals are able to help each other and, at the same time, explore a full range of human relationships that become the material of the drama. AA meets the criteria of what many feel is most important in treatment, 'the assurance of a regular sympathetic hearing, the feeling that somebody is taking one's condition seriously, the discovery that others are in the same predicament, the content of learning that his condition is explicable (which does not depend on the explanations being the right one).' [1]

The quasi religious nature of AA reflected in the films has often been noted and some patients comment on being unable to take the 'religious atmosphere' of **AA**. It can indeed give rise to a certain solemnity and even sanctimonious air about converts portrayed in the film. This criticism is made clear by the heroine of *Days of Wine and Roses* who walks away from her recovered husband unable to accept his new, sober way of life, rather like an unrepentant sinner bravely challenging fate as she walks to perdition.

Being your own man or woman and overcoming drink on your own is not seen as possible in most of these films but there are important exceptions. Some films such as *The Squeeze* and *Rio Bravo* portray heroes who have alcoholism as an obstacle to be overcome, a moral issue which once confronted can be tackled on one's own—anathema to those films which take the view that 'you can't beat this on your own'.

The images of alcoholism conveyed by the media are of loss of control, violence, degradation and loss of reason. These experiences are alien to the majority of alcoholics and yet the image sticks. This may make sufferers afraid of seeking help and indeed patients commonly say that they are surprised that the hospital has no locked doors, no compulsion or confinement, and that apart from their drinking habits, alcoholics look and behave like the rest of us.

Notes

[1] Peter B. Medawar, *The Hope of Progress,* Anchor Books, Garden City, New York, 1973.

Part Three: Drinking on TV

The Representation of Alcoholism on Television

by Edward Buscombe

It seems likely, and I know of no evidence to the contrary, that fictional programmes on television now constitute one of our major sources of 'knowledge' about those areas of society of which we have no direct experience. Thus most people, one assumes, go through life without ever getting to know personally either a criminal or a member of the police force. What they know, or think they know, of crime and the operation of the law will come from programmes like *Z Cars* or *The Sweeney*. And although the sheer numbers of alcoholics suggests that practically everyone will come into close personal contact with one at some time, nevertheless one still suspects that what people know of *alcoholism*, as opposed to individual alcoholics, derives largely from its fictional representation on television. Documentary programmes may play a part, but they are very few in number compared to the scores of fictional characters with drink-related problems appearing on the screen. And, of course, one cannot make the assumption that documentary programmes will necessarily be closer to the truth. Documentaries are made by experts in television, not experts in alcoholism, and the ideas they may bring to bear on the subject may not necessarily be untainted by the myths and half-truths which alcohologists might find in fictional programmes.

That such fictional representations will not often tell us much about the true nature and causes of alcoholism goes without saying. But some closer look at why this should be so might discourage a facile optimism that things can be easily changed, if only the people who make the programmes knew a bit more. One reason has to do with the aesthetics of television. The dominant mode of fiction, the particular variety of realism which characterises practically all British television drama, is ill-adapted to the depiction of explanations of *social* events (which is what I take cases of alcoholism to be). It produces two basic kinds of dramatic character. On the one hand there are the central protagonists around whom the plot turns and who take up most of the screen time. Within the limits of time and money placed upon it, television drama tries to create central characters who are above all individuals, originals who are different from everybody else. Of course they must have enough common humanity in them to encourage the necessary audience identification; but the tendency is for these characters to be special, not typical. And their motivation will be in terms of individual psychology rather than socially determined. Hence if a drink problem is present it will almost inevitably be seen as a character weakness, as a failure in the character's own powers of self-control, rather than as the result of social circumstances.

On the other hand we have characters whose main function is to act as foils for the protagonists, to be plot mechanisms and so on. Here less stress is placed on individuality and more on the construction of an identifiable type. A fidelity to the details of surface appearance is important. Such characters must be true-to-type, life-like in terms of their clothes, speech and general life-style (though in practice being life-like often turns out to mean being like other fictional characters perceived as 'realistic'). Clearly these two categories are not mutually exclusive. Protagonists must also look and speak like 'real people', just as types may be individualised by quirks of character. But just as with the central characters the problem will always be how to find a social explanation, so with the types the difficulty is always to show causes rather than simply effects. Alcoholic types, in order to be recognisable, will be constructed out of the materials already available; but it's in the nature of a type that recognition is the most that can be achieved in the time and space available to a drama. The cause of the condition can scarcely be suggested, except by means of some shorthand reference to an already-'understood' set of circumstances.

But perhaps even stronger than aesthetics in its effects on characterisation is the professional ideology of broadcasters. As far as one can tell, few people involved in the production of television drama series perceive any problems in the representation of social experience. To them television drama series are simply entertainment. It's true that there may be a different attitude towards the single play, which is seen as more 'serious' (see for example the comments of some television writers recorded in chapter 4 of Alvarado and Buscombe[1]); but single plays are less frequent and tend to have smaller ratings.

Insofar as there is a commitment to do anything more than entertain, it would seem to be towards the realism described above, a realism which sees the world as something which is simply and already there and which it is the writer's job to 'reflect'. The writer, according to this view, does not construct an understanding of it in the process of representing it. Rather, he or she captures a pre-existing reality and sets it down. This reality, moreover, is apprehended through direct experience, and not, for example, by the acquisition of other people's knowledge through books. It is therefore not very easy for it to be altered by possibly more correct and objective views of social experience.

In order to earn a living writers must entertain; in order to preserve their self-respect they must try to put things down as they see them—rarely more than that. Television writers, for the most part, simply don't see it as part of their function to increase public understanding of social problems; but even in those rare cases where there is a strong sense of social responsibility there remain difficulties. Writers work in comparative isolation; the machinery, in the sense of organisational structures, scarcely exists which would provide them with any contact with agencies or groups wishing to increase their awareness of social problems.

Other factors within the production system need to be taken into account when seeking to explain why television gives only a very partial representation of social phenomena. Firstly, there is scarcely any way in which those involved in production can test the adequacy of their representations against the audience's own experience. There is an almost complete absence of useful feedback in television from audiences to producers. (See for example Philip Schlesinger, chapter 5[2].) This, combined with the fact that all people, not just writers, who work in television seem to form a tightly-knit social group, means that there are only very limited opportunities for the representations produced to be changed by those who might in fact have more knowledge, or at least an alternative view. Interestingly, this situation appears to be in the course of modification in the United States, where a number of pressure groups have sprung up with the express purpose of changing the representation on television of certain social groups such as blacks and women. Such groups have obviously recognised that these changes will not occur spontaneously within television.

It is in the context of the above remarks that I want to look briefly at the representation of drinking and drink-related problems on one British television drama series. The programme is *Hazell,* produced by Thames Television and transmitted in the first quarter of 1978. The hero, James Hazell, is a Cockney private eye and the ten episodes of the first series recount his adventures through various strata of London life. In the course of these he comes across a number of heavy drinkers, but drinking is not itself the subject of the drama in the case of the supporting characters. Frequently it is merely a plot mechanism, the means whereby the action is triggered. Thus in 'Hazell Settles the Accounts' Cyril Dobson, a crooked accountant, gets drunk in the club where Hazell is working and as a result loses his wallet. Hazell finds it, returns it and is then drawn into involvement with some gangsters. In 'Hazell Plays Solomon' an elderly nurse is sacked for drinking and in revenge switches two babies in the hospital where she works, thus setting in train a mystery which Hazell must solve. For the most part drinking is simply a given element in a character's make-up and no explanation of the condition is offered. Only in the case of Galbraith, a drunken Scotsman who appears in 'Hazell and the Walking Blur', is there a suggestion of a cause. Galbraith is a model of respectability when sober but wild, aggressive and unpredictable when drunk. There is an implication that the repression at work in his sober self somehow causes his outbursts when drinking, and that that repression is the product of his family and cultural background (respectively, a disapproving mother and Scottish puritanism).

But if the drinking of these characters is largely a plot mechanism it is nevertheless interesting to note a pattern in the way that drinking is associated with certain kinds of character. With one exception all the heavy drinkers are failures and their drinking seems to signal a kind of character weakness which is ultimately the cause of their problems. The only character who drinks a lot and is portrayed positively is Hazell's cousin Tel, a jolly Cockney. Tel is not a problem character; or more precisely what might be a problem in other characters (e.g. his fecklessness and hazy moral sense) is treated comically. In Tel drink appears to signify a kind of expansiveness and general zest for life that is almost Falstaffian. What would repay further investigation is why in our culture alcohol can apparently function is such opposite ways, as an index of failure and as an index of zestfulness.

The subordinate characters in *Hazell* are probably typical of many television series. What makes *Hazell* a little different is the central character. Most unusually for a hero, Hazell himself has a drinking problem. In the novels on which the television series was based this problem is quite marked and the background to it sketched in some detail. While in the police force Hazell gets his ankle severely injured. As a result he is invalided out and his distress at losing his job makes him start drinking. The drinking in turn helps break up his marriage. At the time we meet him on television he is starting to put back the pieces of his life, with a new job as a private eye and a determination to conquer his drinking problem.

Both between the novels and the subsequent television series, and within the various episodes of that series, there are some inconsistencies in the delineation of Hazell's drinking problem. In one episode, for instance, it's suggested that Hazell was already drinking heavily while he was still in the police, and moreover that his marriage was at this time already breaking up—whether the drinking was a cause or response to this is unclear. And in some episodes he appears to have decided on total abstinence while in others (e.g. 'Hazell Works For Nothing') he is seen going on a pub crawl. Even within individual episodes there are some strange juxtapositions. Thus in 'Hazell and the Rubber Heel Brigade' there is a scene (discussed in more detail below) in which Hazell meets his former wife in a pub and refuses a drink on the grounds that he has given it up. Yet the immediately following scene shows him opening and helping to consume a bottle of wine. Unless we are to suppose that wine isn't really drinking there's some odd characterisation going on here. What such inconsistencies seem to suggest, though, is that the programme as a whole lacks a coherent model of alcoholism. One is entitled to believe that this lack results not just from the fact that the television scripts were mostly written by writers other than the authors of the original novels and the fact that since some half a dozen writers contributed to the ten scripts televised not all of them knew exactly what the others were doing. Rather, the incoherence results also from what has already been said about the nature of television drama generally. Hazell's character wasn't invented in order to inject some colour into a treatment of the problem of alcoholism; it was, rather, the other way round.

In one sense the treatment of the problem is perhaps not novel. Perhaps one reason why heroes so rarely have a drinking problem is that while drinking in itself may be manly, drinking heavily is seen as indicating a lack of inner strength, strength which by definition a hero must possess. And although Hazell does have such a problem, by the time we meet him he has more or less got it under control, certainly after the first episode. It's notable too that this control has been arrived at by the use of his own resources of character. Hazell, like a true hero, doesn't need anyone's help.

But two aspects of the way the central character is treated do seem to offer a genuine contribution towards understanding, rather than the mere circulation of received ideas. Firstly, there is a short scene in 'Hazell Plays Solomon' where Dot, an older woman for whom Hazell does occasional jobs, reproves him for getting sexually involved with a client whom he is then forced to betray. Hazell, unable to face himself, has got drunk. Dot is scornful of such a response: 'Found yourself a moral dilemma, have you? I suppose you adopted the classic male solution and went out and got legless.' And while Hazell has been feeling sorry for himself Dot has more or less solved the case.

The scene, though modest in its ambitions, neatly punctures the male machismo of drunkenness, identifying and at the same time subverting a connection between Hazell's behaviour and a more general, not simply individual, condition. It's also Dot who remarks to Hazell in another episode, when Hazell makes a comment on her own drinking, that 'there's nothing more boring than a reformed piss-artist'. This comment can be seen in the context of a scene in 'Hazell and the Rubber Heel Brigade' where Hazell meets his former wife in a bar. As he sips his tomato juice she comments that she's glad to see he's got his drinking under control. But from his general demeanour it's clear that control of his drinking has not solved his problems, that the removal of the drinking has left merely a void. The point is rather harshly made by his wife, clearly still a little bitter: Hazell, trying to brighten things up, tells her that he's got a new car. 'I'm glad you've got something,' she replies. This glimpse into Hazell's state of mind after his 'cure' is a rare instance of television series drama seeing a drinking problem as more than a simple matter of strengths and weaknesses of character.

'From his general demeanour it's clear that control of his drinking has not solved his problems' (Hazell, Thames Television, 1978).

Rare because, firstly, of the comparative complexity of the scene, which manages to suggest that Hazell's new car is a substitute, and an inadequate one, for his drinking; that his wife while approving his feat of giving up knows him (and perhaps people generally) sufficiently well to realise that he hasn't thereby solved the problems which drove him to drink in the first place, and that Hazell himself knows this and that talking about the car is merely ill-disguised bravado (all this, I think, comes over from the way the scene is played; on paper there is merely the potentiality of these meanings). Rare too because in television and the cinema generally the 'cure' is all too often seen as a magic event. If it works everything is happy ever after. The situation of the reformed alcoholic whose life, while more manageable, is also emptier is one which the media have not much explored. Perhaps it would simply be too depressing. And rare, finally, because the kind of television we have, the restraints imposed by limitations of time, by demands for strong heroes supported by a gallery of types, and by the isolation of the production situation all make it difficult to explore beyond stock responses to any social problem.

Notes

[1] M. Alvarado and E. Buscombe, *Hazell: the making of a TV series*, BFI/Latimer, 1978.
[2] P. Schlesinger, *Putting 'reality' together: BBC News*, Constable, 1978.

Drinking and Drunkenness in *Crossroads* and *Coronation Street*

by Roger King

This is a book on the media and alcoholism. Its critical concern will, I assume, be the way in which the problem of alcoholism and the character of the alcoholic has been presented in film and, to a lesser extent, in television. But for a student of the media in general, and of television in particular, rather than an alcohologist, it is the absence of alcoholism rather than its presence as content which seems of central importance. This is not of course a unique example of television apparently failing to deal adequately and responsibly with a *social problem*. In precisely the same way as television soap opera shows a world of alcohol without alcoholism, so it also shows a world of cigarette smoking without terminal cancer, and sex without venereal disease.

Yet the paradox is nevertheless sharper in the area of alcohol than in the other two areas: smoking and sex are both areas where the television authorities deliberately exercise restraint in showing the activities. While, on the contrary, in soap operas such as *Coronation Street, Crossroads* and *Emmerdale Farm* not only, at the crudest level of analysis, does a lot of drinking appear to take place; but more importantly, licensed premises, whether a pub or the bar/reception area of a motel, form an important location for the series, and a focal centre for the series' characters. Characters meet round the bar, conflicts arise and resolve, new characters and new narratives are introduced over a drink, gossip is exchanged.

We must at this point be extremely careful in not claiming that this is innovatory on the part of television itself. British television developed soap opera out of sound radio and The Bull in Ambridge is the direct ancestor of the Rovers Return and the *Crossroads* motel. The notion of the pub as a valued social focus for a local community has a long and respectable tradition in English intellectual culture, in the nineteenth century social realist novel of Dickens, George Eliot, and Hardy, as well as Orwell in his albeit partially ironic *Evening News* article 'The Moon Under Water',[1] and the justly celebrated work by *Mass Observation,* published as *The Pub and the People.*[2] We must not hold television responsible for the creation of myths which they have not invented, but merely perpetuate and reinforce. But at the same time, the perpetuation and reinforcement of these myths has two definite social effects. Firstly, they are disseminated to mass audiences, at least in the case of soap operas such as *Crossroads* and *Coronation Street.* And secondly, by presenting pubs, drinking and alcohol in one particular way these programmes effectively prevent alternative views and attitudes gaining equal currency. This continually present idea of normal everyday drinking in turn may partially explain the absence of alcoholism on television.

In this paper I shall argue that precisely the importance of *Coronation Street* and *Crossroads* is the way in which essentially mythical views of drinking are presented. But first of all, it is necessary to understand what we are defining by the term myth itself (a concept which I have derived here broadly from the work of Roland Barthes in general, and in particular from his essay 'Myth Today').[3] The first prerequisite of this is evident already—it is a collective, rather than an individual view or attitude, anonymous rather than attributable to a single author. I am nowhere claiming that the attitudes to alcohol revealed in these programmes are innovatory; they are inherited, not created. Secondly, a myth is coherently organised and structured; the mythological structures of *Crossroads* and *Coronation Street* include alcohol—indeed, alcohol is an important element of them, much more important than, say, smoking and certainly as important as sex—but alcohol remains only one element of those structures, and is absorbed by them. Thirdly, a myth, to exist effectively *as* a myth, *must* be believed to be true. To take a crude example: Father Christmas exists as a myth, if you believe in him. Once you have stopped believing in him, he is a fairy story or a lie (or a means by which economic wealth is distributed across generations within a nuclear family). I am arguing that in these three senses, the meaning of soap operas and their presentation of the world conforms to the concept of myth.

To take our three criteria in turn. On one level, it is obvious that *Crossroads* and *Coronation Street* are collective, rather than individual, productions. They are collaborative enterprises. But this collaboration exists also in time: previous writers and producers, previous narratives, define and constrain contemporary possibilities for innovation. Soap operas are in this sense limited and constrained by their own longevity.

Secondly, we have asserted that in both *Crossroads* and *Coronation Street* drinking is assimilated into an integrated structure: it derives its meaning from the form and content of the programmes as a whole. It does not exist as a separate disembodied entity independent of the programmes' concerns, setting, and emphases. Later in the paper, I shall suggest that the difference between the two programmes has important implications for the way in which drinking is presented. But at this point, I wish to return to, and develop, the third criterion, that of credibility.

Both *Crossroads* and *Coronation Street* are experienced as essentially realistic. Both series work, as do soap operas in general, by creating the illusion of a real continuous living social world of which the viewer is a regular participant. This realism is confirmed by the regular programming of both series: we 'make our visit' to *Coronation Street* or *Crossroads* at set times and days in the week; only in exceptional circumstances (e.g. the World Cup, the Olympics) are they dislodged from their traditional slots. Realism is further reinforced by their longevity, and by the publicity and marketing of individual actors and actresses from both series. As far as the audience is concerned the gap between actor and role has been eliminated.

But to the programmes themselves. We have already stressed the identity of their form: they are *soap operas,* they are both presented as realistic, they are both marketed similarly, during peak-viewing hours for mass audiences. They also share a similar narrative structure—a loosely interwoven mesh of separate *stories* involving in one case the inhabitants of a mythical Salford street, in the other, the staff of a West Midlands motel. There are, even at this level, marginal differences: the narrative texture of *Coronation Street* is denser than *Crossroads,* and is (generally) less melodramatic in its selection of separate *stories.* But the real differences lie elsewhere; and since this paper is addressed to the particular examination of drinking, rather than to a detailed comparison of the two programmes, these differences will necessarily be stated rather briefly.

The world of *Coronation Street* is (or is seen to be) predominantly working-class, the world of *Crossroads* predominantly middle-class. The central characters of *Coronation Street* purport to be the inhabitants of an urban working-class terraced street; the central characters of *Crossroads* are the two business partners who own a motel, and their employees. It is the families of the owners whom we know most intimately rather than the families and friends of the employees. And at the same time, the viewer is permanently aware of the centrality of the employer/employee relationship which maintains the motel.

Secondly, the world of *Coronation Street* is static, while the world of *Crossroads* is mobile. *Coronation Street* is a haven of stasis in a world of urban development, characters seldom leave, new characters are seldom introduced. The *Crossroads* motel, on the other hand, exists to serve a geographically and

'Coronation Street, *we might say, is social in its definition of crisis,* Crossroads *psychological'* (Crossroads, ATV, April 1978).

socially mobile world. Pop stars, millionaires, and magnates stay a few nights, initiate a *story*; and leave, to be replaced by others. In the series as a whole this is paralleled by the mobility of the staff: cooks and waitresses leave and are replaced; as well as receptionists, gardeners and garage mechanics. So that the mobility is not simply the product of the setting of a motel—it is central to the programme as a whole.

To bring these two differences together, we might say that the overriding difference between the two programmes is between a *Coronation Street* which is essentially collective in its emphasis, and a *Crossroads* which is essentially individualistic. This difference defines the different type of individual *stories* which are the narrative basis of the mesh the series provide. Put simply, these individual *stories* move from crisis to resolution: typically a *Coronation Street* story involves a collective crisis, a conflict between two individual Street characters, which is resolved by a mutual resolution of the conflict; one accepts defeat, or a compromise is reached. In *Crossroads,* crisis is seldom represented by a socially realised conflict of this type. It is, rather, an individual problem—remorse, guilt, frustration—which is resolved (often with the help, it is true, of a sympathetic friend) by a personal decision, by getting (or giving up) a job, by moving away, by leaving a wife or husband. *Coronation Street,* we might say, is social in its definition of crisis, *Crossroads* psychological.

It is within these different mythological structures that drinking is presented in both programmes; it derives its meanings differently from its mythological context.

Nowhere is the collective nature of *Coronation Street* more explicit than in the use of the pub, the Rovers Return, which is the focus of drinking in the series.

Of course, drinking takes place elsewhere, including at home. Stan and Hilda Ogden take the odd bottle of beer back, Annie Walker offers the occasional sherry in her parlour behind the bar, Ken Barlow produces a bottle of wine when he entertains in the evening. But these exceptions only reinforce the normative function of the pub. Ken Barlow and Annie Walker are pre-eminently characterised by their exceptionally bourgeois lifestyles. Barlow via his college education and experience of schoolteaching, Annie by her tenancy of the pub itself and by her social pretensions. The Ogdens are equally marginal; their domestic drinking signals their general fecklessness and inadequacy.

Self-evidently the pub operates as the communal centre of the Street—occasionally, the series offers us alternatives: the Mission Hall, the Community Centre, or the Cabin Tearoom. But the pub operates permanently and continuously as the public gathering place for the inhabitants of the Street. Of course, in one sense, this is entirely realistic: one function of the English pub is that it does precisely operate as a social centre. But in *Coronation Street* this function of the pub is reinforced by a range of strategies which mythologise its cohesive nature.

Firstly, the Rovers assimilates characters who, if acting to realistic type, would certainly disapprove either of alcohol as such, or would not be permanent and consistent users of pubs. Ena Sharples, with her long commitment to Evangelical religion, playing the harmonium at the Mission Hall, or the late Ernest Bishop, Evangelical preacher, have had their permanent place in the Rovers, Ena for her milk stouts in the snug, Ernest his half a pint and pie at lunchtime. The Rovers is so powerful in its mythological ability to operate as a socially cohesive and integrative setting that it will assimilate those characters who realistically would be in the Temperance Movement.

At the same time, the Rovers is an arena where realistic, divisive working-class social conventions cease to exist: women drink alone and order drinks themselves without incurring hostility or negative comment. Similarly we are seldom aware of hostility to teenage drinking, nor to any legal problems surrounding under-age drinking. Young and old, male and female, are all made welcome at the Rovers.

The Rovers, then, breaks down rather than confirms social distance. It operates to reduce the possibility of social conflict. This is communicated to the viewer in several specific ways.

Firstly, we are never clear, even as permanent viewers, how many bars the pub has. There is a snug, sometimes but not always inhabited by Ena Sharples and perhaps Albert Tatlock, but it is not a consistently employed part of the set. The ultimate effect of this is to stress the social equality of the pub: when characters enter the Rovers they drink in one bar as equals. The Rovers, unlike

'Coronation Street, *we might say, is social in its definition of crisis,* Crossroads *is psychological'* (Coronation Street, Granada, April 1978).

67

a real pub, does not confirm social inequality in the structure of its bars. One source of social conflict is thus eliminated.

The other major source of social conflict that is eliminated in the Rovers Return is that between staff and customers. This is communicated in several ways. Firstly, the bar staff, Bet and Betty, live on the Street as equals to their customers; they serve their neighbours. Secondly, in purely physical terms, conversations take place as much across the bar as in front or alongside it (the lack of tables further emphasises this). But the most significant strategy by which potential conflict between staff and customers is eliminated is by the almost total absence of the economic dimensions of brewing and public houses. True, we know that the Rovers sells Newton and Ridley beer, and that Annie Walker is a tenant, not a manager. Indeed, the aspect of the suitability of a woman tenant has been employed more than once in the narrative of the series. But we know nothing of costs, the quality of the beer, in short of any consumer complaints. We seldom see the brewer's dray or the pie van deliver their goods. The Rovers Return will be the last pub in England to be affected by CAMRA.

The pub assimilates all in the Street; and offers an arena for social integration. This is reinforced by its curiously restrictive quality. Although a few extras are occasionally glimpsed playing darts in the background, it is a pub where no thirsty traveller ever finds himself ten minutes before closing. The real pub in the real world serves a geographically mobile world; the Rovers is a haven of social stasis, untouched by mobility. This is symptomatic of the programme as a whole; it is a curiously carless street, and the infrequent use of location filming outside the Street reinforces the claustrophobic immobility of the programme. People seldom go on holiday (and if they do, the viewer does not go with them). A day trip is an adventure.

But if the Rovers exists in a world of geographical stasis, its temporal limits know no bounds. For the pub never closes. Or never appears to. It is always populated, and the viewer is never clear whether it is lunchtime or evening. We know when the pub has just opened; but we seldom know whether it is about to close. Although purporting to be a realistic corner street pub, the Rovers exists in both mythological space and mythological time, untainted by the economic dimensions of the modern brewing industry.

Thus the Rovers Return provides the ideal setting for the resolution of the conflicts which arise in individual narrative *stories*; in *Coronation Street* drinking is, on the whole, associated with the convivial resolution of conflict—it is presented as a social collective activity, and affirmed, as it were, as part of the community of the Street.

By comparison, the bar of the *Crossroads* motel is singularly impoverished. Not that the viewer is unaware of its existence near the reception area—as indeed we are also not unaware of the sherry decanter in Meg Richardson's lounge, or the Martini bottle in Diane's flat. Drink is shown to be available in *Crossroads*, at the motel, or in individual homes. But it does not lubricate the bearings of the social machine in the way that it does in *Coronation Street*. In fact, despite its insistent visual availability, far less alcohol is consumed by *Crossroads* characters than by *Coronation Street* characters. But that is not the most significant difference; when drinking does take place in *Crossroads,* it tends to be a lonely asocial experience, a signal (for other characters and the viewer) of individual crisis, rather than a sign of the social resolution of it.

In order to demonstrate these differences, and to provide examples of them, we monitored closely all *Coronation Street* and *Crossroads* episodes for the month of April 1978, and selected two sequences from both as being representative of both series' treatment of alcohol as a whole: the *Coronation Street* extract consists of a sequence from the 12 April episode, the *Crossroads* extract of a sequence from 18 April.

Characteristically, both extracts consist of a narrative structure which interweaves several *stories.* In the *Coronation Street* extract four separate stories are brought together, and the pub provides the arena for their possible resolution. Firstly, Bet, the barmaid, has overstayed her welcome living with Alf and Renee Roberts over the grocery shop. Alf and Renee are embarrassed about broaching the matter to her. But in the extract of 12 April, in the pub, Bet apparently resolves the problem by announcing that she is looking for a flat. The resolution proves to be premature, however, and over a later drink, Bet explains that she has refused the flat since it was in such a lamentable condition.

Secondly, Bet has also stirred Hilda Ogden's suspicions that her husband Stan is having an affair. In the sequence of 12 April, Bet attempts to resolve the crisis by demonstrating to Hilda how she sprayed perfume on Stan as a joke in a previous episode. Hilda remains unconvinced.

In both these individual stories, then, the pub provides a potential, but not finally successful, resolution of two conflicts. The remaining two stories are resolved more successfully.

The third individual story concerns Mavis, who serves in the newsagent's and tobacconist shop managed by Rita Fairclough and owned by her husband Len. She has had a row with her boy friend Derek, who has attempted to make it up by sending flowers. This has had no effect on Mavis, who remains inconsolable, but in this sequence Rita persuades her to at least accompany her to the pub, where she and Len also celebrate the resolution of the fourth story. Len has previously been arrested on a drunk and disorderly charge—he fears for the professional reputation of his building firm. In the episode of 12 April, all is saved, and a new contract secured: the pub provides the natural arena for the celebration of this success.

In the *Crossroads* extract of 18 April, three stories are juxtaposed. Firstly, Jim Baines, a mechanic at the motel, is in hospital. His wife has been befriended by Mr. Lee the garage manager: a sexual affair has possibly developed from this, and she has received an abusive poison-pen letter. In the 18 April episode she visits her husband in hospital in order to show him the letter, taking with her a propitiatory bottle of Guinness. Meanwhile, in the bar of the motel, Sharon (who also works in the garage) has a gin-and-tonic, while waiting to console the understandably worried Mr. Lee with a drink.

In the second story Chris, David Hunter's son, while previously studying at the Sorbonne, has been blackmailed by his girl friend Simone into joining an international terrorist group, and become involved in a kidnapping plot.

The third story is equally fraught. Diane, waitress/receptionist/hairdresser at the motel, suspects that a friend (and a girl friend also of a police constable) is a thief. But lines have become crossed, and in the sequence of 18 April, the police constable arrives in Diane's flat suspecting her of being a thief. The misunderstanding is not resolved in the subsequent conversation—and no drinking takes place. Yet the visual presence of Diane's bottle of St. Raphael on her sideboard tray is apparent to the viewer.

We must not force the evidence of these two extracts too far; but the general differences seem immediately clear. Drinking is a more insistent activity in *Coronation Street*; it is confined to the pub, it is collective in its nature. In *Crossroads,* one sequence of drinking takes place in the motel bar, but the other two take place in a hospital ward and a private lounge respectively. And although (apart from Sharon drinking her initial gin-and-tonic) characters do not drink alone, only one partner in each setpiece actually drinks. Jim Baines' wife offers the Guinness to him, but she does not drink with him. David Hunter offers Simone a brandy, but again he does not drink himself. Drinking is not the social activity that is so heavily emphasised in *Coronation Street.*

Neither is it associated with the resolution of social conflict as it is in the *Coronation Street* extract. Of course, it must be pointed out that in this particular sequence not all the current conflicts are finally resolved: of the four separate stories, only one—the securing of Len's new contract—is permanently settled and celebrated. Mavis' antagonism to Derek is delayed rather than solved, and the two stories involving Bet await later resolution—but characteristically when they in turn are brought to a successful conclusion in subsequent episodes, it is in the pub over mutual drinks that it takes place.

In the *Crossroads* episode, on the other hand, drinking is associated with crisis itself. Jim's wife presents him with a drink to enable him to deal psychologically with the crisis she is about to present him with through the poison pen letter. Simone's drink signals her potential threat to David Hunter: it confirms to the viewer her unreliability and deceitfulness. Hunter's refusal to drink equally signals his ability to cope with the potential crisis.

But perhaps most significantly, the one episode which appears to move towards a possible resolution of a misunderstanding—the discussion between Diane and the policeman—is conducted over a coffee although alcoholic drinks are shown to be available. In *Coronation Street* this would most certainly have taken place in the Rovers over a few drinks.

I have claimed that the two episodes concerned are representative of the two series as a whole. Inevitably, the above has sharpened rather than elided the differences between them. *Crossroads* occasionally does employ the motel bar in a similar way to the Rovers Return; the manual staff—Carney the gardener and nightwatchman, the garage mechanics—do sometimes use the bar as the equivalent of a pub. But this is comparatively rare. Similarly, it would be misleading to suggest that *Coronation Street* does not occasionally—and selfconsciously—acknowledge that drinking can be problematic. Len's drunk and disorderly charge is an indication of this; but it had been incurred while celebrating the impending marriage of Alf Roberts, and the blame for the incident partially shared by his wife Rita for refusing to allow him home. So the incident was presented very ambiguously—and although as viewers we were expected to condemn his abuse of the policewoman who arrested him, in the extract of 18 April we are equally expected to share the triumph of his return to normal business.

So to summarise: drinking in both *Coronation Street* and *Crossroads* derives its meaning and emphasis from the different mythological structures of the programmes. In *Coronation Street* it is predominantly a convivial, collective, integrative activity—it is rooted in the pub as an arena of sociability, and associated with the resolution of social conflict. In *Crossroads*, on the other hand, it is shown as abnormal, isolated, individual, and associated with crisis itself, with the inability, temporary or permanent, to cope with emotional and psychological pressures, with instability and unreliability. In *Coronation Street*, drinking signals harmony, in *Crossroads* disintegration.

It is at this point that a student of the media must hand over to the professional alcohologist and health educationalist. The effects of the media on individual behaviour are complex and the subject of unresolved dispute. Neither is there a simple answer to the question as to which view of drinking is the socially most responsible or indeed accurate. The society in which we live, its economic institutions and its culture of ideas, art and literature have been responsible for our inheriting both views of alcohol and its social usage: they were not invented by television. In our real lives, we use drink in both ways, as a means of social integration, and as a mean of coping with psychological crisis. This chapter has served its purpose if it has demonstrated that the way in which drinking is presented by the media is not as simple as it may at first appear, even in the most apparently realistic programmes such as *Coronation Street* and *Crossroads*.

Notes

[1] Reprinted in Sonia Orwell and Ian Angus (eds.), *Collected Essays, Journalism and Letters of George Orwell*, 4 vols., London, 1968.
[2] John Sommerfield and Mass Observation, *The Pub and the People*, Seven Dials Press, 1971.
[3] See Roland Barthes, *Mythologies*, Jonathan Cape, 1972.

Part Four: Afterword and Filmography

Afterword: what are the implications?

by Mike Lewington

Richard Dyer's chapter 'The Role of Stereotypes' concludes that the role of the alcoholic stereotype is the same as that of other stereotypes in so far as they allow what is in effect a continuum of behaviour to be divided into what is normal and safe, and what is abnormal and dangerous. In the case of the alcoholic stereotype this entails a division of the spectrum of drinking behaviour into harm-free and harmful drinking through, in this instance, a particularly graphic image of the effects of the latter. People thus 'know' that they are drinking in a harm-free fashion as long as they do not take on the features of the stereotype. Whilst in theory this dividing line might be located anywhere between teetotalism and chronic self-poisoning, what is particularly important from the alcohologist's point of view is that it is located so far into the area of severe damage. That is to say, much drinking behaviour that would be perceived as lying in the area of harm-free drinking is from the clinical point of view extremely harmful. The area in which this issue is particularly important is that of physical damage. In the films and television programmes viewed the physical sequelae of alcohol abuse figure little, if at all, whilst the social (skidrowism) and psychological (craving, loss of control, dependence) effects are focused upon in their extreme forms. It is well established that chronic excessive alcohol consumption will produce a range of physical effects not necessarily accompanied by manifestations of dependence and social damage. The currency of the stereotype, along with popular notions that alcoholics are in some special way different from everybody else, effectively militates against a situation in which, by having a broader conception of what constitutes an alcohol problem, people might easily recognise the harmful effects of their drinking as being caused by their pattern of consumption.

Andrew Tudor's chapter 'Alcohol and the Mystique of Media Effects' stresses the need for a sophisticated model of media effects. He notes that there exists in our culture a pool of ideas and concepts which are utilised in the interpretation of the world and the construction of reality. An idea or concept not found within this pool is in a very real sense unthinkable. The idea of inconceivable concepts has been demonstrated by anthropologists in 'primitive' societies, but is it the case that in our late-capitalist pluralist society there is much left that is inconceivable?—one can precisely never know. Nonetheless a small refinement to Tudor's analogy crystallises its relevance: in the conceptual pool some of the ideas are nearer to the surface than others, and are utilised by both media and public alike as most 'meaningful' and non-problematic. Thus the continual rearticulation of the alcoholic stereotype entails a range of other possible representations becoming by inverse proportion less visible in the gathering sedimentary mud. Thus the alcoholic stereotype gains its power not only from its continual reiteration, but also through the absence of contending or different representations.

The subtlety of this 'indoctrination by omission' can be seen in the case of *Coronation Street*. Roger King's elucidation of the mythopoeic nature of the series emphasises that social phenomena occur therein without harmful consequences. To all intents and purposes there is continuous harm-free consumption. One might pause to wonder, if someone was shown as having a drinking problem in the series, whether it would in fact be inevitable that they were represented in stereotypical fashion, at least in terms of their being special or different, since by not doing so, by showing harmful drinking developing out of harm-free drinking, the entire ethos of the programme would be undermined by introducing an ambiguity into our attitude to the Rovers Return.

It would therefore seem to be the case that the task of health education must be to undermine the alcoholic stereotype and create a climate in which the public's notion of harmful and harm-free drinking is more congruent with the scientific evidence. This might be achieved through a deliberate confrontation of the stereotype, or through the promotion of a range of other representations.

Edward Buscombe in his chapter 'The Representation of Alcoholism on Television' comments on the difficulty of inducing change through the education of writers and producers, noting that the media tend to see their current mode of representation as being unproblematic, or having no effect, or being just entertainment. Thus, short of coercion, it would seem more likely that in the short term any transformation will be effected not through the 'public entertainment' media but through the traditional methods of communication available to health educators. These include short films which are shown in cinemas and very late at night on television. Buscombe's reminder that films and programmes featuring alcohol problems are made by writers and producers and not by experts in alcoholism also holds true, though less obviously so, for health education films. If such films are to be effective, they must be free from covert messages which refer to different models of alcoholism than the one being promoted in the film and consequently undermine it. Filmmakers are likely to be influenced by traditional ways of representing alcoholics on film and may not necessarily be aware of the dissonance created by the utilisation of elements of those representations. The extent to which stylistic conventions drawn from these filmic representations can undermine a contending representation is worthy of consideration.

Bruce Ritson in his chapter 'Images of Treatment' notes that in his clinical experience patients are often surprised at the non-custodial nature of an alcoholism treatment unit. The images of treatment in films and television programmes reflect and reinforce certain expectations in the public mind. Similarly the contrast evident in many films between the punitive, custodial and ineffec-

73

tive hospital and the warm, personal and successful approach of Alcoholics Anonymous tends to reinforce the popularity of the view that AA is the most appropriate agency from whom to seek help. Whilst it may be true that AA has enabled a great many people to achieve sobriety, it is also the case that many people find its methods and goal (total abstinence) unacceptable. That there is a range of other agencies who might respond to an individual with a drinking problem with a variety of treatment methods and goals seems generally unknown.

This book has attempted to open the debate which will lead to a fuller understanding of the relationship between the public's and the media's images of alcoholism. A more complete understanding will only be achieved through rigorous analysis of the modes of representation in every medium and through careful analysis of the notions about alcoholism and treatment held by the general public. This understanding should enable strategies to be devised with the aim of reducing the gap between belief and scientific knowledge.

Filmography

by Jim Hillier

This filmography consists of brief credits and notes (with an indication of their contemporary reception where possible) on fifteen films which were screened for the National Film Theatre Season, Representation of Alcoholism: Booze in the Movies, in London, September, 1978. In no sense is it an attempt to compile a comprehensive listing of films dealing with alcoholism and/or drinking.

What Price Hollywood?

USA 1932. Dir. George Cukor. Prod. David O. Selznick. With Constance Bennett, Lowell Sherman. Prod. Co. RKO. 88 mins.

What Price Hollywood? is the first 'version' of the *Star is Born* story, following the rise to stardom of a young actress in Hollywood, paralleled by the decline and downfall through alcoholism of her mentor, a film director. A typical male alcoholic—initially urbane, later losing self-respect—the director is the prototype for the tragic Norman Maine character in Cukor's 1954 *A Star is Born*, though lacking the structural complexity of the later characterisation. The depiction of the movie-going public is more savage than in the 1954 film, with the star's career wrecked by the scandal of the director's suicide. The world of Hollywood is juxtaposed with 'the messy, uncomfortable subject of alcoholism'.

Vessel of Wrath

GB 1938. Dir./prod. Erich Pommer. With Charles Laughton, Elsa Lanchester, Tyrone Guthrie, Robert Newton. Prod. Co. Mayflower Pictures. 95 mins.

Against an 'exotic' colonial background, this comic morality drama plays out a sexist (and racist) fantasy in which indulgent sensuality (Charles Laughton seducing native girls and drinking to excess) and puritan restraint (Elsa Lanchester and Tyrone Guthrie as a missionary and reverend doctor) are first in opposition and then shown as being capable of synthesis. The sting in the tail: with Laughton 'civilised' and Lanchester 'humanised' the couple return to England to run a country pub together, each to display in moderate form the qualities/faults previously associated with the other.

The Lost Weekend

USA 1945. Dir. Billy Wilder. Prod. Charles Brackett. With Ray Milland, Philip Terry, Jane Wyman, Howard Da Silva, Prod. Co. Paramount. 95 mins.

An archetypal study of the male alcoholic loved by a devoted woman but

75

nonetheless needing to drink as compensation, here for lack of creativity as a writer. The action of the film is largely devoted to tensely 'realistic' observation of the central character's strategems to get money, and his drinking bouts. An early example of the 1940s 'social problem picture' cycle, *The Lost Weekend* was praised for its 'realism', its detachment, its general seriousness of purpose: 'an example of what Hollywood can do when it is used by a good director' (*The Spectator*); 'uncompromising . . . without gloss' (*The New Statesman*); 'an unrelenting, uncompromising study of alcoholism' (*Daily Sketch*); 'shatteringly realistic' (*New York Times*). Though these assessments might appear less just with hindsight—realism being, after all, a matter of changing conventions—they were clearly likely to produce, given the critical establishment's privileging of realism and its deep-seated distrust of Hollywood, less favourable judgements on later films in which alcoholism was dealt with in more overtly formal ways, such as melodrama (see, for example, *Too Much, Too Soon; I'll Cry Tomorrow*). *The Lost Weekend* is a crucial film simply because it provided the model or reference point from which almost all subsequent films about alcoholism—certainly all Hollywood films—were judged: it is rare to find a review of later films about alcoholism which does not make some reference to it.

Smash-Up: A Story of a Woman (British Title: *A Woman Destroyed*)

USA 1947. Dir. Stuart Heisler. Prod. Walter Wanger. With Susan Hayward, Lee Bowman, Marsha Hunt, Eddie Albert. Prod. Co. Universal-International. 103 mins.

One of many 1940s' 'problem pictures', *Smash-Up* attempts to relate alcoholism to women's social roles: 'Don't call me names—until you know why I do such things' ran the promotion line. The central character, Angie, abandons a singing career to marry an unknown singer-songwriter whose later success deprives her of the roles of wife and mother as well as of her career and edges her into alcoholism. Appearing two years after *The Lost Weekend,* the film was inevitably compared and found lacking, being judged as corny and soggy. Two things are notable about the film's reception in Britain. First, there was general agreement that the sight of a drunken woman was, as the *News Chronicle* put it, 'incomparably more disgusting' than the sight of a drunken man; one review began: 'Among the most unpleasant things Hollywood exports is the sight of a drunken woman.' No reviewer stopped to ask why this deeply ingrained prejudice should exist. Second, the film's melodramatic stylisation, running counter to the accepted canons of 'realism', led to crushingly literal comment on the film's attempt to deal with the effects of women's enforced social-sexual roles.

Key Largo

USA 1948. Dir. John Huston. Prod. Jerry Wald. With Humphrey Bogart, Edward G. Robinson, Lauren Bacall, Lionel Barrymore, Claire Trevor. Prod. Co. Warner Bros. 100 mins.

A thriller morality in which the moral superiority of the Bogart character is pitted against the physical superiority of Robinson's gangster, holding siege to an isolated hotel during a hurricane. The presentation of the woman alcoholic (Claire Trevor) functions as an index of the gangster's contempt for human values. She displays a gamut of alcoholic symptoms and is 'cured' by shifting allegiance to the Bogart character from the gangster. Almost without exception Trevor's role and performance as the gangster's alcoholic moll was liked more than any other performance, for example: '. . . the one character who does stand out is the aging moll, played by Claire Trevor, who gives a beautifully judged impression of a faded show girl, broken by her life with the gangster, and a slave of the bottle' (*Daily Mail*). Given the general antipathy of reviewers to women alcoholics on the screen, it can be speculated that this role is acceptable at least partly because the character is placed as unthreatening, beyond accepted values, and, importantly, also a dramatic ploy, a source of pathos, in relation to the male characters rather than as a dramatic focus in herself.

Harvey

USA 1950. Dir. Henry Koster. Prod. John Beck. With James Stewart, Josephine Hull, Charles Drake, Cecil Kellaway. Prod. Co. Universal-International. 104 mins.

Interesting as one of the few attempts to deal humorously with drinking, *Harvey* is potentially subversive in trying to present non-conforming excessive drinking as a positive escape from a stultifying society. At the same time, it can be argued that the light-hearted presentation of the people who try to 'cure' the amiable drunk of his hallucinatory companion, a six-foot white rabbit, takes the sting out of his rejection of them. In 1950 the film found little favour among critics, largely because it seemed to operate outside the recognisable, and largely assumed, norms of either obviously realistic or obviously fantastic representation. One review touched upon the film's interest: 'Which of us is sane? The realistic, crude, down-to-earth go-getter, or the man to whom the creatures of his imagination are more real than the world around him? *Harvey* will leave you wondering. Most people now know the basic story of the successful stage play on which this film version was based, the tale of a gentle, unworldly inebriate who ambles through life in the company of an enormous white rabbit (Harvey) existing only in his own imagination. James Stewart, whose amiable, gawky, dithering and shy smile make him the ideal choice for the eccentric Dowd, puts over his philosophies with such endearing and persuasive charm that one is in danger of seeing the invisible Harvey' (*Reynolds News*).

Come Fill the Cup

USA 1951. Dir. Gordon Douglas. Prod. Henry Blanke. With James Cagney, Phyllis Thaxter, Raymond Massey, James Gleason, Gig Young. Prod. Co. Warner Bros. 110 mins.

A study of alcoholism within the context of an involved narrative concerning the newspaper business and gangsters. The 'cures' offered the Cagney and Gig Young characters are a contradictory amalgam of then current treatment orthodoxies: the alcoholic must first reach rock bottom; practical aid can wean people off drink; common sense psychology is preferable to psychiatry. The press reception of the film was heavily marked by disturbance at a film which mixes its genres; for example: 'Somewhere in this version of another *Lost Weekend* have been lost a gangster story, a newspaper story, a love story and an old buddies story. Even such sober fellows as the Warner Brothers cannot escape the ravages of drink! Having liberally sprinkled their script with alcohol they stagger uncertainly from one plot to another' (*Evening Standard*). Elsewhere the film's seriousness was perceived: 'Not as studiously disillusioned as *Lost Weekend* and its message somewhat blurred by a subsidiary plot, the film nevertheless makes a sincere attempt to analyse the tragedy of alcoholism, stressing particularly that it is a disease, and that no emotional appeal or sound argument can reach its bearer. A look into the abyss is the only cure' (*The Spectator*).

Come Back Little Sheba

USA 1952. Dir. Daniel Mann. Prod. Hal Wallis. With Burt Lancaster, Shirley Booth, Terry Moore, Richard Jaeckel. Prod. Co. Paramount. 99 Mins.

Interesting for its presentation of alcoholism both as a retreat from the failure to match up to the cultural mores of middle-town America (family, success, etc.) and as a guilty secret to be hidden from that culture. Beneath the overtly optimistic ending—the central character's wife and Alcoholics Anonymous will always be there to shield him from despair—lies a bleaker vision: as a retreat from an unbearable reality alcoholism is too potent a lure ever to be medically and socially contained. Despite the addition of some alcohol-problem scenes to William Inge's stage play (an AA meeting, a hospital scene after a drinking bout), *Come Back Little Sheba* was not perceived at the time as being at all centrally about alcoholism. Contemporary reviews stressed the drama's realism, contrasted with usual Hollywood fare, and Shirley Booth's performance, constructing through pathos what the trade press called the film's 'compelling woman's angle'. Thus, the film's reception tended to ingore the particular—alcoholism, social pressures—and emphasise the universal—human frailty, courage, stoicism, compromise. Lindsay Anderson, in *Sight and Sound*, was far from untypical: '*Come Back, Little Sheba* is a poignant picture of a situation near despair—the Delaneys' is the sort of relationship that carries on quietly in one corner of a Chekhov play. The sharpness of perception and the tenderness to human frailty which is implicit throughout (particularly where the people are growing old and unattractive; the healthy young are most obnoxiously characterised) express a sadly stoical attitude, a subdued affirmation of the values of courage and affection. (It is essentially about the sad business of making the best of a bad job.) These are far from the traditional qualities of commercial cinema. . .'

A Star is Born

USA 1954. Dir. George Cukor. Prod. Sidney Luft. With Judy Garland, James Mason, Jack Carson, Charles Bickford. Prod. Co. Transcona Enterprises for Warner Bros. 154 mins.

The central story concerns the rise to stardom of the Judy Garland character but inextricably linked to this is the story of her alcoholic husband, a declining film star, presenting the alcoholic as tragic hero, fatally flawed and inexorably impelled towards self-destruction. The character remains sympathetic, partly because his drinking is never explained (though the pressures of Hollywood are implied), so that the wife's return to stardom on his name after his death is emotionally right. Most reviewers of the film concentrated on Garland's bravura come-back performance, but Mason's performance and role as the husband were commented upon interestingly by several reviewers, indicating the degree to which the character is presented and received, in many ways typically for male alcoholics, as urbane and charming, though doomed and self-destructive; for example: 'a drunk though he was, he made the character always likeable. One sensed the man's fight against his urge' (*Sunday Dispatch*). But this was also the heyday of psychological explanations for problems and although such explanations in movies were usually derided, their *absence* in *A Star is Born* was noted with some puzzlement, for example in the *Daily Telegraph*: 'He has wit, he is capable of a cynical, burnt-out chivalry, and James Mason gives him a full measure of good looks and effortless charm. What then is eating the man? We never know. It seems strange that in Hollywood, where child-stars have psychiatrists and psychiatrists have psychiatrists, nobody has been able to diagnose his trouble. Insecurity as a toddler? Or just the insecurity that troubles all those who, like Arthur Miller's salesman, teach nothing and make nothing but spend their lives "up there riding on a smile and a star"?'

I'll Cry Tomorrow

USA 1955. Dir. Daniel Mann. Prod. Lawrence Weingarten. With Susan Hayward, Richard Conte, Eddie Albert, Jo Van Fleet. Prod. Co. MGM. 119 mins.

Lillian Roth's 'story of suffering and degradation'. Encouraged to drink but punished for being an alcoholic, Roth's alcoholism is presented as stemming from an overbearing mother pushing her to professional success (itself presented as somewhat 'unnatural' for women), and from losing a man. Typically for the 1950s, Alcoholics Anonymous is instrumental in Roth's recovery, but not before abject degradation. The film's reception was marked by several typical attitudes. It was regarded as Hollywood again indulging in lurid sensationalism, for example: '*I'll Cry Tomorrow* like *The Snake Pit* (lunacy) and *The Man With The Golden Arm* (drugs) is Hollywood cashing in on human suffering under the guise of giving us a Social Document and an Awful Warning' (*Evening News*). Typically, women alcoholics were less acceptable than male and the heavily psychological explanations common in the 1950s were ridiculed, *The Times* commenting that 'few Hollywood films today are complete without Freudian arguments about the responsibilities and sins of the parents'. Also unsurprisingly for the time, Alcoholics Anonymous was perfectly acceptable as the plot vehicle allowing for Roth's final recovery, though its dramatic effectiveness here was doubted.

The Buster Keaton Story

USA 1957. Dir. Sidney Sheldon. Prod. Robert Smith, Sidney Sheldon. With Donald O'Connor, Ann Blyth, Rhonda Fleming, Peter Lorre. Prod. Co. Paramount. 91 mins.

An example of Hollywood's fictionalised biographies of spectacularly flawed stars, this tells the story of Buster Keaton, the great silent film comedy star. The film is interesting because its threadbare production values combined with its emphasis on Keaton's private rather than professional life clearly expose its unproblematic use of accepted and simplistic beliefs about alcoholism; for example, that the immature personality buys drink when power cannot be bought. In particular the seemingly implausible happy ending mirrors the then current orthodoxy of Alcoholics Anonymous.

Too Much, Too Soon

USA 1958. Dir. Art Napoleon. Prod. Henry Blanke. With Dorothy Malone, Errol Flynn, Efrem Zimbalist Jr, Ray Danton. Prod. Co. Warner Bros. 102 mins.

Very much of the 1950s in both its uneasy blend of melodrama and realism and its heavily psychological explanations, *Too Much, Too Soon* tells the biographical story of Diana Barrymore, from failed stage actress, to Hollywood, to alcoholism after the death of her father, her alcoholism explained as due to personality flaws, failed parental relationships and inability to live up to the Barrymore name. Typically, John Barrymore's 'creative' male alcoholism is contrasted with his daughter's sordid female alcoholism (sexual excess, emotional sterility and immaturity). The film was generally received with the usual disdain reserved for Hollywood melodramas, especially the more sensational kind, but the hostility which greeted the film can also be seen to come from a clear (though unreflected) distate for the representation of women, as opposed to men, alcoholics—given special force in this case because John Barrymore had come to represent a dominant type of the male alcoholic—doomed, fatally flawed, but 'saved' by charm, looks, talent, wit. The *Daily Mail* review (by Fred Majdalany) implied all of these responses and is particularly interesting for its assumption that women alcoholics *naturally* called for forms of representation befitting their gender: 'In one field I think women would do well to avoid equality with men. I have in mind alcoholism. There is something formidable and tragic about any alcoholic but the female variety is really terrible.

Nothing more fatally draws attention to this than a film having as its heroine a lush—as the Americans describe a lady afflicted with this malady—unless it is animated by a spirit of compassionate inquiry, intelligent analysis or art. *Too Much, Too Soon* betrays no traces of any of these things . . .'

Rio Bravo

USA 1959. Dir./prod. Howard Hawks. With John Wayne, Angie Dickinson, Dean Martin, Ricky Nelson. Prod. Co. Warner Bros. 141 mins.

Rio Bravo's plot concerns a group of men holed up in a Western town trying to guard a villain until the US marshal arrives. One of the men, Dude (played by Dean Martin, whose screen characters have often been drunks or heavy alcohol users), is an alcoholic former deputy who, by becoming involved in the action, is restored to sobriety. Thus, alcohol, which flows freely in most westerns, becomes an element of plot, but the director's interest is not at all in any faithful depiction of the condition of alcoholism or drunkenness, but rather in the need for personal self-respect and maturity. Dude's drunkenness is simply explained as caused by an unhappy love affair and 'simply' overcome, in Dude's rehabilitation, by the exercise of will and control, thus offering an interesting example of alcoholism used as a structural dramatic device rather than as something of interest and concern in itself. John Wayne's sheriff offers an uncompromising model –through his controlled drinking among other things–to which Dude must aspire.

Days of Wine and Roses

USA 1962. Dir. Blake Edwards. Prod. Martin Manulis. With Jack Lemmon, Lee Remick, Charles Bickford. Prod. Co. Warner Bros. 116 mins.

The world of 'work' with its enforced socialising and that of 'home' with its enforced isolation are both shown as being initially pleasantly stimulated by drink, then dependent upon it, and finally wrecked by it. The film succeeds in handling subtly shifts of mood—from farce, through high seriousness, to melodrama—which reflect the complex range of attitudes, from indulgence to disgust, in society towards the different stages of drinking. *Days of Wine and Roses* provoked a clear division of response among reviewers. Most considered it a serious attempt to deal with alcoholism, for example Philip Oakes in *The Sunday Telegraph:* 'It is difficult to pinpoint precisely when the film drunk ceased to be a laughing matter . . . but *Days of Wine and Roses* gives good and sufficient reasons for the joke being over. Alcoholism, it says flatly, is a disease. There are no funny drunks, no romantic drunks, no charming drunks: just sick drinkers who are steadily, and compulsively soaking away their lives. . . . The public confessions at AA meetings, the downbeat ending, the transformation of PR smartie into shaky convalescent—all these are a far cry from the cosy conventions of earlier films on the same subject.' Other reviews attacked the film, thus *The Daily Worker:* 'It's not however the nightmare hell of *Lost Weekend* or *Come Back Little Sheba.* It's the romanticised torment of those tidily done-up problem people who respond with weekly regularity to treatment by Dr. Kildare.'

The Squeeze

GB 1977. Dir. Michael Apted. Prod. Stanley O'Toole. With Stacy Keach, David Hemmings, Edward Fox, Stephen Boyd, Carol White, Freddie Starr. Prod. Co. Martinet Productions for Warner Bros. 107 mins.

Little is offered to 'explain' the central character's alcoholism, which has cost him both wife and job, and it functions as an element of drama, rather than a theme to be explored, within the overall structure of this taut thriller: will he withstand the strain of trying to rescue his kidnapped wife and child or lapse into drinking? Given this role of alcoholism in the film, it is not surprising that no 'explanations' are offered, that the representation of the treatment process is fantastic and that engagement in the action seems to restore the character's self-respect, and perhaps to 'cure' him. In other words, since alcoholism is merely a dramatic element, one way of propelling the narrative, rather than something to be examined closely and seriously, its representation refers more substantially to earlier dramatic representations than to current knowledge and practice.